Christian African Americans

A Journey from Biblical Times to Today

Rene' Stanley

Books By Rene'

Contents

Part IV

Modern Movements

Rene' Stanley

Introduction

A Long, Bright Thread

Christianity did not arrive in Africa with European ships. It was already there—in royal courts, desert monasteries, bustling ports, and city schools—long before colonial powers drew maps. This book follows that long, bright thread: from an Ethiopian treasurer reading Isaiah on a desert road, to the libraries of Alexandria and the courtrooms of Carthage; from the rock-hewn churches of Ethiopia and the frescoed cathedrals of Nubia, to hush-harbor songs in the hold of a ship; from brush arbors and gallery pews to independent Black churches, mass meetings, and modern megachurches; from abolition sermons to civil-rights strategy, from liberation theology to today's hybrid, digital, global congregations.

What this book aims to do:

Tell a big story in clear, terms

Correct the common myth that African Christians "borrowed" a foreign faith

Show how African and African American Christians built enduring institutions, shaped theology, and remade public life

Honor both the famous names and the everyday people whose prayers, ledgers, and labor held communities together

How the book is written:

You'll find storytelling and history side by side. Chapters open with scenes you can see and hear—a chariot rolling through heat haze, a ring shout pulsing through a ship's hull, a choir steadying a frightened crowd—and then set those moments in their real historical context. The language is plain. The arguments are grounded in evidence: scripture, inscriptions and coins, archaeology, church minutes, newspapers, sermons, letters, and oral histories.

What you'll encounter

Ancient roots: Alexandria's schools, North Africa's theologians (Tertullian, Origen, Athanasius, Augustine), Ethiopia's royal conversion, and Nubia's thousand-year Christian kingdoms

Atlantic crossings: the "invisible church" of enslaved people, spirituals as scripture in song, sacraments in fields and rivers, and the quiet genius of women who kept faith alive

Institution building: free Black congregations, schools, mutual-aid lodges, newspapers, banks, clinics, and the Social Gospel in growing cities

The freedom struggle: churches as headquarters for boycotts, voter drives, legal defense, and nonviolence training—a movement with a steeple

Thinking it through: liberation and womanist theologies naming God's solidarity with the oppressed, and the church's call to repair structures, not only souls

Today's landscape: megachurch scale and scrutiny, digital worship, immigration and global ties, environmental justice, mental-health ministry, debates over gender and sexuality, and the next generation's "belonging before believing"

Why it matters now

This story changes how we see both Africa and America. It shows:

Christianity in Africa is ancient, creative, and foundational to the faith's development.

Black churches did not simply "respond" to history; they made history—building schools, banks, hospitals, newspapers, and movements for freedom.

Theology is not only written in books; it is sung, organized, and lived—at altars, in kitchens, on picket lines, and in city halls.

How to read this book

Straight through from Acts to AI.

Or dip in by interest: ancient Africa (Chs. 1–4), medieval Nubia (Ch. 5), slavery and the "invisible church" (Chs. 6–8), institution building and abolition (Chs. 9–11), the Social Gospel to civil rights (Chs. 12–13), liberation theology (Ch. 14), and the 21st century (Ch. 15).

Use it for group discussion. Each chapter raises clear, practical questions—about memory, justice, worship, leadership, and hope.

A note on words and places

"Ethiopia" in the Bible can mean regions south of Egypt; in this book it often refers to the ancient kingdom of Aksum (in modern Ethiopia and Eritrea).

"Kush/Nubia" refers to ancient kingdoms in what is now Sudan and southern Egypt.

I capitalize "Black" to honor a shared history and culture, and "African" to name a vast, diverse continent and diaspora.

When ancient or local titles appear (Candace, Kandake, Baqt), they explained them in context.

What this book is not

It is not a textbook full of jargon.

It is not a church manual telling you what to believe.

It is not a romantic tale that skips hard truths. It faces violence, injustice, and failure honestly—and notices repair, endurance, and joy with equal care.

Sources you can trust The story rests on many kinds of evidence: the Bible and early church histories; coins, inscriptions, and murals from Aksum, Faras, and Dongola; slave narratives and plantation ledgers; church covenants, minutes, and newspapers; court records from rebellion and civil-rights trials; sermons and letters; and modern scholarship.[1]

A gentle content note Some chapters describe enslavement, war, lynching, and other harms. I will not dwell on pain for spectacle, and will not look away. I will keep real people at the center and treat their faith, struggle, and dignity with respect.

An invitation Whether you are a believer, a skeptic, or simply curious, you are welcome here. You do not need to share the faith to follow the story it tells. It is a human story, carried by mothers' boards and monks, treasurers and teenagers, bishops and bricklayers, by people who kept minutes and sang through storms. It is the story of a faith that is not just a private feeling but a public way of life—with addresses, budgets, names, and songs strong enough to teach courage to children not yet born.

Begin where you like. If you want a single doorway, start with Chapter 1's desert road. Watch an African official climb out of a royal chariot and into the water. That splash still echoes. The thread he carried runs through every page that follows.

PART I

ANCIENT AFRICAN CHRISTIANITY

Books By Rene'

Chapter 1

Africans in the Bible

The desert road stretched endlessly southward from Jerusalem, its ancient stones baked white under the midday sun. Dust devils danced in the distance where the rocky hills of Judea gave way to the vast emptiness that led toward Gaza, toward Egypt, toward the heart of Africa itself. It was here, on this desolate stretch between the holy city and the ancient world beyond, that two men would meet and change the course of Christian history forever.

The chariot appeared first as a shimmer in the heat haze, its wheels raising a small cloud of dust that hung in the still air. As it drew closer, the magnificence of the vehicle became clear—this was no merchant's cart or traveler's wagon, but the royal conveyance of a great kingdom. Ebony wood inlaid with ivory and gold caught the sunlight, while silk curtains in deep purple rippled gently in the chariot's wake. The horses were Arabian stock, their coats gleaming with the care that only royal stables could provide.

But it was the man seated within who truly commanded attention. Dark-skinned and dignified, he wore the fine linen robes that marked him as a person of extraordinary importance. Gold bands encircled his wrists, and a signet ring bearing the seal of his authority glinted on his finger. This was a high-ranking court official of Queen Amantitere of Kush, administrator of the entire royal treasury.

In his lap lay a scroll of the prophet Isaiah, its Hebrew characters carefully inscribed on papyrus that had cost more than most men earned in a year. The treasurer's lips moved silently as he read, his brow furrowed in concentration. He had made the long journey north to Jerusalem for the festival of Pentecost, drawn by a spiritual hunger that his position and wealth could not satisfy. Now, returning to his duties in distant Meroë, he carried with him copies of the sacred writings—the Torah, the Prophets, the Psalms—treasures more precious to him than all the gold in the royal treasury.

The passage that held his attention spoke of suffering and vindication:

> "Like a sheep he was led to slaughter,
> and like a lamb before its shearer is
> silent, so he did not open his mouth. In
> his humiliation justice was taken from
> him. Who can describe his posterity?
> For his life was taken away from the
> earth." Acts 8:26-40[2]

Who was this mysterious figure Isaiah described? The treasurer had pondered this question throughout his journey, consulting with rabbis in Jerusalem, debating with fellow pilgrims, searching the scriptures for understanding.

As the chariot rolled southward, he was unaware that another traveler moved along the same route. Philip the evangelist had been preaching in Samaria when an angel of the Lord commanded him to go south on the desert road to Gaza. Without hesitation, Philip had obeyed. Now, as he walked under the blazing sun, he caught sight of the royal chariot ahead. "Go over and join this chariot," the Spirit whispered in his heart.

Philip quickened his pace, running alongside the moving vehicle. The sound of a voice reading aloud reached his ears—Hebrew words spoken with the careful pronunciation of one who had learned the sacred tongue as a second language. As he drew closer, Philip called out: "Do you understand what you are reading?"

The chariot slowed, then stopped. The treasurer looked down at this dust-covered stranger with curiosity rather than annoyance. "How in the world can I," he replied, "unless someone guides me?" With a gesture of hospitality that would have astonished those who knew only of African wealth but not of African grace, he invited Philip to climb into the chariot beside him.

As Philip settled onto the cushioned seat, the treasurer pointed to the passage that had captivated his attention. "Please tell me," he asked earnestly, "who is the prophet saying this about—himself or someone else?"

Beginning with this very scripture, Philip proclaimed the good news about Jesus. He told of the carpenter from Nazareth who fulfilled Isaiah's vision, of the crucifixion that looked like defeat but was actually victory, and of the resurrection that conquered death itself. As the chariot rolled on, two men from different worlds discovered they served the same God.

Then, as they crested a small rise, the glint of water appeared ahead. The treasurer's heart leaped with sudden understanding. "Look, there is water!" he exclaimed. "What is to stop me from being baptized?"

Nothing, Philip realized. Not his African origin, not his foreign accent, not even his status as a eunuch—a condition that would have barred him from full participation in Temple worship. The gospel of Jesus Christ knew no such boundaries. Both men descended from the chariot, and in the cool water of the desert spring, Philip baptized him.

When they came up out of the water, the Spirit of the Lord suddenly caught Philip away. The new Christian stood dripping in the spring, gazing at the spot where Philip had vanished, then threw back his head and laughed with pure delight. He had come to Jerusalem seeking God and found Him in the most unexpected place.

Climbing back into his chariot, the royal treasurer commanded his driver to resume the journey south. He was returning to Africa not merely as an administrator of gold and silver, but as a bearer of infinitely greater treasure. The good news of Jesus Christ would travel with him to the court of Queen Amantitere and the bustling markets of Meroë, a kingdom whose sophistication and power are well-attested by archaeological evidence.

As the chariot disappeared into the southern horizon, carrying its precious cargo of newfound faith, the desert settled back into its ancient silence. But the reverberations of this encounter would echo through the centuries. Christianity had found its way to Africa not through conquest or colonization, but through the genuine spiritual hunger of an African seeker who encountered the risen Christ on a dusty road. This was how it began—with Africa reaching out to embrace the faith that would flourish on the continent for the next thousand years and more, producing some of the faith's greatest theologians and most magnificent churches.

Historical Context: The Kingdom of Kush and the Power of the Candaces

The chariot that carried the treasurer southward from Jerusalem was returning to one of the ancient world's most formidable kingdoms. Far from being a peripheral backwater, the Kingdom of Kush represented a civilization that had thrived for over a thousand years, ruled mighty pharaohs, defeated Roman legions, and accumulated wealth that made it legendary throughout the Mediterranean world. To understand the significance of the Ethiopian treasurer's conversion, we must first grasp the extraordinary power and sophistication of the African kingdom he served.

Stretching from the First Cataract of the Nile at Aswan southward into the heart of what is now Sudan, the Kingdom of Kush had established itself as a major force in Northeast Africa by 750 BCE. Its capital at Meroë, located some 200 kilometers northeast of modern Khartoum, controlled the vital trade routes that connected sub-Saharan Africa with the Mediterranean world. Gold from Nubian mines, ivory from the African interior, exotic animals, ebony, and iron goods flowed northward through Kushite ports, while Mediterranean luxuries, ideas, and technologies moved south.

But it was the remarkable institution of female rulership that made Kush truly unique in the ancient world. The title "Candace"—from the Meroitic word *Kandake*—was not a personal name but a royal designation meaning "Queen Mother," "Queen Regent," or "Royal Woman." While male kings also ruled Kush, the Candaces wielded extraordinary authority, commanding armies, conducting diplomacy, and governing vast territories with skill that earned the respect even of their enemies.[3]

The archaeological record reveals the names and achievements of eight major Candaces who ruled between 170 BCE and 314 CE, spanning the entire period of early Christian expansion. Queen Shanakdakhete was the first to rule independently, breaking new ground for female sovereignty. Queen Amanishakheto was buried with such lavish grave goods that her tomb became legendary for its opulence. But it was Queen Amanirenas who demonstrated most dramatically the power of the Candaces. When Roman forces invaded, she led a successful military campaign, conquered territory, and forced Emperor Augustus to negotiate an equal peace treaty.[4]

The story of Queen Amanirenas reads like legend yet is thoroughly documented. When the Roman prefect Gaius Cornelius Gallus annexed traditional Kushite territory around 27 BCE, Amanirenas waited for the moment when Roman forces would be distracted elsewhere. That opportunity came when Augustus deployed his legions to Arabia, leaving Egypt lightly defended.[5]

Striking swiftly, Amanirenas led an army northward, recapturing disputed territories and pushing into Roman Egypt itself. She seized Elephantine, Syene, and Philae, taking Roman prisoners and plunder. She ordered the bronze head of a statue of Augustus buried beneath temple steps as a symbolic act of defiance.

The Roman counterattack drove Kushite forces back but could not break their resolve. The Greek historian Strabo described Amanirenas as "a masculine sort of woman and blind in one eye," the injury said to have been sustained in battle.[6]

For five years the war dragged on, draining Roman resources and demonstrating Kushite resilience. Finally, in 21 BCE, Augustus met with Kushite envoys, agreeing to a peace that involved Roman withdrawal and a pledge not to tax Kushite lands, affirming Kush sovereignty.

The political and cultural world of the Ethiopian treasurer was thus powerful and sophisticated. Most scholars identify Queen Amantitere as the Candace mentioned in the book of Acts, based on chronological alignment. The royal court at Meroë was cosmopolitan, with Greek, Meroitic, and Egyptian languages spoken and trade items from across the Mediterranean commonplace.

The treasurer, highly educated, had access to Hebrew scriptures and Jewish religious traditions common among the Jewish communities in the Nile Valley and the great library at Alexandria. The royal treasury he administered reflected enormous wealth from gold mines and trade routes. In this environment, African religious traditions coexisted with growing Jewish and Christian influences, creating a world open to spiritual exploration.

Biblical Africans Beyond the Ethiopian Eunuch: Simon of Cyrene and Early African Presence

While the Ethiopian treasurer's conversion held immense significance, other African figures appear in the biblical narrative. Simon of Cyrene, compelled to carry Jesus's cross, reveals an early African presence in Jerusalem at the time of the crucifixion.

The Synoptic Gospels record Simon's role concisely. Mark notes Simon's origin as Cyrene, an important North African city with a large Jewish diaspora. He is identified as the father of Alexander and Rufus, suggesting their family was known within the early Christian community.[7]

Cyrene was a major hub of Jewish life, with pilgrims traveling to Jerusalem regularly for festivals. Simon likely belonged to such a group or resided in Jerusalem.

Paul's letter to the Romans mentions a Rufus, who many scholars believe was the same son of Simon, indicating the family's ongoing involvement in the Christian movement.

Early Christian interpretation saw Simon's carrying of the cross as a model of discipleship, an act embraced rather than resented. The presence of other African figures like Lucius of Cyrene, a leader in the Antioch church, further emphasizes Africa's early and foundational role in the Christian story.

Early Church Father Interpretations: African Voices on African Stories

The significance of these biblical figures is amplified by the Church Fathers who interpreted their stories, many of whom were themselves African. John Chrysostom praised the Ethiopian treasurer's spiritual hunger and royal status, emphasizing Christianity's universal reach.

Tertullian, from Carthage, coined the term "Trinity" and shaped foundational Christian doctrines from an African perspective, often challenging Roman imperial authority. Augustine of Hippo influenced the course of Western Christianity more than any theologian after Paul, and his work was deeply reflective of his African cultural experience. Origen of Alexandria pioneered biblical interpretation in a multicultural context, connecting the gospel to the wider world of Greek philosophy.

These great thinkers did not simply receive doctrine; they were primary architects of Christian theology, bringing their unique African cultural insights to the developing faith.

The African Foundation of Christian Faith

The meeting of Philip and the Ethiopian treasurer was part of a larger pattern revealing Christianity's African roots from its inception. From Simon of Cyrene to influential theologians like Augustine and Tertullian, Africa was not a passive recipient but an active architect of the Christian faith.

When the treasurer returned south, he carried the gospel not to a "dark" continent of colonial imagination, but to powerful kingdoms rich in culture, intellect, and influence. The theological contributions of the African Fathers established a tradition that would flourish in African kingdoms and influence Christian theology for centuries.[8]

This foundation makes it clear that when enslaved Africans in the Americas embraced Christianity, they were in many ways reconnecting with an ancient African Christian tradition, not merely adopting a foreign faith.

The journey continues in the next chapter with the rise of Alexandrian Christianity, the first great African center of Christian learning and thought outside of Palestine.

Chapter 2

Alexandria: Christianity's First Great Center

The Crucible of Cultures: An Introduction to Ancient Alexandria

Around the year 60 CE, the port of Alexandria was not merely a city, but the vibrant, chaotic heart of the Mediterranean world. Founded nearly three centuries earlier by Alexander the Great, it was strategically placed at the mouth of the Nile, a perfect bridge between Africa, the Middle East, and the burgeoning Roman Empire. For a traveler arriving by sea, the first sight would be the legendary Pharos lighthouse, one of the wonders of the ancient world, its beacon guiding ships laden with grain, gold, spices, and silk into the bustling harbor.

From its inception, Alexandria was defined by its multiculturalism. It was a city where Greek was the language of the street, but the gods of Egypt were still worshipped in ancient temples. Here, Roman administrators governed a population of native Egyptians, influential Jewish merchants, Persian traders, and scholars from every corner of the known world. By the first century CE, it was one of the largest and most important cities in the Roman Empire, second only to Rome itself.

This African metropolis was the undisputed intellectual capital of the age. Its Great Library and the Mouseion research institute were magnets for the era's greatest minds, from the geographer Ptolemy to the philosopher Plotinus. But just as important as its secular learning was its religious diversity. Traditional Egyptian gods were venerated alongside the Greek pantheon. Judaism thrived in well-organized synagogues, and within this complex tapestry of faiths, small, nascent Christian groups were beginning to emerge.

One of the city's most influential communities was its large and deeply rooted Jewish diaspora. For centuries, Jewish life had flourished in Alexandria, creating a powerful center of learning that was both Greek in language and Hebrew in faith. It was the scholars among these Alexandrian Jews who produced the Septuagint, the first major Greek translation of the Hebrew Scriptures, making the sacred texts accessible to a wide, literate audience across the Mediterranean and creating the very version of the Old Testament that most early Christians, including the apostle Paul, would use.[9]

This dynamic environment—a city where African, Jewish, and Hellenistic values merged—proved to be the fertile ground where Christianity would transform from a small Palestinian sect into a global faith capable of engaging with the great philosophical questions of the day. Alexandria's unique blend of cultures was the crucible of theological innovation, and it was here that Christianity found its first great center outside of Palestine, beginning its journey toward becoming a truly universal faith.

The Arrival of a New Faith

The sandal strap snapped on the cobblestone of Alexandria's streets. A traveler from the coast—short-bearded, dusty—stepped into a shoemaker's stall near the Canopic Way. When the awl slipped and pierced Anianus's hand, the craftsman cried out the city's old creed, "Heis ho Theos"

("God is one"). The traveler, Mark, took the wounded palm, prayed quietly, and wrapped it. Pain went away. In the hush that followed, the talk turned—as it sometimes does, when accidents disclose intentions—from mending leather to mending the world.

> The oldest account remembers the moment plainly. "When the strap was torn," writes Eusebius, Mark "healed him by calling on the name of the Lord," and "Anianus, persuaded by the word, was baptized" and "entrusted with the care of those in Alexandria" when Mark withdrew for a time; Eusebius dates Anianus's succession to "the eighth year of Nero." 10

> Alexandria provided fertile soil: for generations, its sizable Jewish community—recorded by Philo—cultivated a practice of reading Scripture as a layered text, always looking beneath the surface for deeper meaning. They read the Law in Greek (the Septuagint) and argued that God's revelations moved through layers: story on the surface, wisdom beneath. Such habits mattered. When the news of the crucified and risen Jesus reached this harbor of priests and philosophers, it met a people already trained to hear meaning at more than one pitch.[11]

At first the word traveled along familiar lines: through diaspora synagogues, among those who shared Scripture and calendar. But markets are borderless. Greek-speaking dock hands and clerks heard the message in the idiom of Plato and the Stoics; native Egyptian families, who still left bread at old household shrines, found the title "Soter"—Savior—both strange and fitting. In the lanes near the shipping offices, one heard the new blessing—"Peace to you in the Lord"—and soon saw it copied on receipts and private notes. The city had a way of turning words into currents and sending them far.

As the gathering grew, so did its seriousness. House meetings became assemblies; visiting teachers stayed longer; copied scrolls passed hand to hand. There is no single founding charter for what came next—only the sense that in Alexandria the mind was part of the soul's worship. What began as catechesis—teaching for new believers—settled into a curriculum: language, memory, logic, Scripture, and prayer under one roof.

Archaeological finds back up those memories. In the eastern quarters and the insulae near the harbor, under later Roman and late-antique layers, excavators found what look like early Christian meeting places: crosses scratched into walls, niches for lamps, and casual Greek invocations of the Kyrios carved by ordinary hands — everyday marks of a group coming together. These remains appear in local spots tied to the shops south of the main colonnade, strengthening the case that Christians met in domestic, not just public, spaces.[12]

The Alexandrian Mind

When Pantaenus took the charge of the school, the city gained a teacher who could quote Zeno at noon and Moses by moonrise—a former Stoic who repurposed philosophy's discipline for catechesis and mission. Students who came for argument stayed for prayer.[13]

Clement of Alexandria widened the frame. He gathered sayings like a bee gathers nectar, and in Stromata he argued a bold thesis: "Philosophy" was "a covenant" or "preparation" granted to the Greeks, just as "the Law" was to the Hebrews, so that "the philosophy of Christ" might be received without violence to truth discovered before. [14]

Origen, Clement's most brilliant student, pressed further. He wrote as a man who believed reality has grammar. "God is simple and without body," he insists; one must "think of God as a simple, intellectual nature," not imagine him "as a body bounded by size." Scripture, too, demands a mature reader: "The divine Scriptures have a body, a soul, and a spirit." The literal sense where it edifies; the moral for the soul's healing; the spiritual where the text itself invites ascent. Under his hand, the Exodus becomes not only Israel's march through sand but the soul's passage from bondage; Eden, not only a garden of earth, but a parable of dignity and risk. Allegory, for Origen, is not a license to float above history; it is a discipline for reading history toward God. [15]

> This method met Alexandria's questions head-on. If God is one, how can Christians adore Father, Son, and Spirit without rending unity? If God is incorporeal, how can the Son be truly seen and known? If Scripture pricks the conscience in one place and exalts it in another, how does one read without breaking faith? The school forged tools to bear those weights. Later formulas—"begotten, not made," "of one essence with the Father"—would name what had been long implied in Alexandrian classrooms: the Son is no creature in time, but the eternal Wisdom and Image of the Father; the Spirit is no created breeze, but giver of life. [16]

Their students became missionaries with libraries, pastors who could parse a participle, confessors who could face prison without losing their taste for books. They read Isaiah with philosophers and Christ with psalmists; they learned that the same God who formed reason formed mercy, and that orthodoxy without charity is a gong without a hand.

African Roots and Influence

Alexandria's brilliance did not float above Africa; it grew from it. The city fed on the Nile's patience and the desert's silence. When Christians in Egypt prayed in their own tongue—Coptic hymns rising from mud-brick chapels—the Scriptures sounded like home. Icons gave Mary a local mother's eyes; angels stood like temple guards whose stances the elders recognized. In Upper Egypt and across the first cataracts into Nubia, the ancient art of reading meaning in form—lotus and wing—met a new conviction that the cross gathers symbols like the river gathers streams.

Leadership matched the soil. Origen, African-born and city-schooled, taught with a rigor that astonished his peers. A generation later, Athanasius made the city's courage famous, compressing the school's labor into a line: "God became man that man might become god." Five times emperors pushed him out; five times the African church received him back.[17]

Ideas moved outward on the same routes that brought grain to Rome. Allegorical reading found adherents in Caesarea and Rome; the Alexandrian habit of squaring Scripture with the best of philosophy gave apologists something better than slogans. Even where Antioch preferred a tighter literal sense, the debate itself proved the export: Alexandria had made interpretation the church's public work.

Archaeology at Kom el-Dikka, a late-antique academic quarter, shows an active teaching culture. Excavations found stepped auditoria with stone benches, apsidal (semi-circular) teaching niches, and nearby lecture spaces. These built features point to organized, public teaching in the city, a setting into which Christian instruction would have fit naturally.

Alexandria's Enduring Legacy

Set between river and sea, Alexandria became the crucible where three inheritances met: the Jewish genius for Scripture, the Greek discipline of reason, and the African instinct for symbol and community. Clement could say without embarrassment that "philosophy was a preparation for Christ"; Origen could insist that God is "without body" and that Scripture has a "body, soul, and spirit" ; Eusebius could name dates and bishops without apologizing for precision. Out of that meeting rose a Christianity capable of bearing questions without panic, reading texts without violence, worshiping God with mind and heart.[18]

For roughly three centuries, the "mind" of the church—its schools, debates, and early creeds—thought in patterns born on African soil. It was natural, then, to look west along the coast. Another city—Carthage—would take the Latin tongue and hammer it into doctrines and defenses that set the West's cadence for a millennium. There, Tertullian would coin the very legal-leaning words by which the Trinity would be confessed; there, Augustine would give the church a soul it still recognizes. Alexandria taught the church to think; Carthage would teach it to argue and to pray in another register. The river becomes the sea.

Chapter 3

The African Theological Giants

Tertullian of Carthage: The Father of Latin Christianity

In the sun-scorched streets of ancient Carthage, the air hung thick with the smells of baking bread, exotic spices from eastern caravans, and the salty tang of the nearby Mediterranean. The sharp cries of merchants haggling in a dozen different tongues mingled with the rhythmic clang of blacksmiths forging tools and weapons. It was in this vibrant African metropolis, a crossroads where Roman law met Punic resilience and Greek philosophy clashed with local traditions, that Quintus Septimius Florens Tertullianus—a man poised to change the very language of Christian faith—was born and educated.

Raised in the second century as the son of a Roman centurion, Tertullian received the finest classical education Carthage could offer, becoming a master of rhetoric and, most crucially, Roman law. His early career as a lawyer in the city's bustling courts trained him not just in persuasion, but in the art of relentless argumentation: how to construct an unassailable case, anticipate and dismantle objections, and wield the power of the written word like a weapon. This legal training would become the defining characteristic of his theological work, providing the intellectual architecture for a new, robust form of Latin Christianity.

After a profound conversion experience, Tertullian turned his formidable skills from the courtroom to the church, becoming its most passionate and articulate defender. His writings are not gentle meditations; they are fiery, meticulously constructed legal briefs against heresy, paganism, and imperial injustice. This is most evident in his masterpiece of defense, the *Apologeticus*. Presented as a formal legal appeal to the Roman governors, it systematically demolishes the slanderous accusations leveled against Christians. With the precision of a prosecutor, he turns Roman legal principles back on the empire itself, arguing that its persecution of Christians was not only immoral but illegal. It is here that he pens his most defiant and memorable declaration, a phrase that captures the paradox of faith under pressure: "The blood of the martyrs is the seed of the church." He argues that the state's violence, meant to crush the movement, only served to fertilize its growth.

Tertullian's legal genius reached its zenith in his battle against the heresy of Monarchianism, a teaching that blurred the distinct identities of the Father, Son, and Holy Spirit. In his treatise *Against Praxeas*, he single-handedly forged the theological vocabulary that would become central to all of Western Christianity. He was the first to use the Latin term *trinitas* (Trinity) to describe the nature of God, explaining this profound mystery with the clarity of a legal statute: "The mystery of the dispensation is still guarded, which distributes the Unity into a Trinity, placing in their order the three Persons—the Father, the Son, and the Holy Ghost."[19]

To build his case, he drew directly from the language of the Roman courts. He introduced the term *substantia* (substance) to denote the single, shared divine essence of the Godhead. To explain the distinct identities within that unity, he deployed the crucial legal term *persona* (person). In Roman law, a *persona* was not a "personality" but a legal entity with distinct rights and standing. With this, Tertullian could argue that the Father, Son, and Holy Spirit were three distinct "persons" who nevertheless shared one divine "substance." He explained the balance with unassailable logic: "As if in this way also one were not All, in that All are of One, by unity (that is) of substance; while the mystery of the dispensation is still guarded."

These precise legal terms provided the church with a robust framework to articulate a doctrine that was both mysterious and rational. His work was not just theological abstraction; it was forged in the intense crucible of North African culture—a place where Roman imperial power, indigenous African heritage, and the Christian faith intersected and often clashed. The intensity in his writings reflects the fervent spirit of a man grappling with faith under the gaze of an often-hostile empire.

His legacy as the father of Latin Christian literature is unparalleled. Through his legalistic rhetoric and theological ingenuity, Tertullian shaped the Christian imagination for centuries. His life and work stand as a powerful testament to the intellectual vitality of North African Christianity, proving that the continent was not a passive recipient of the faith, but a primary forge where its most enduring doctrines were hammered into shape.

Origen of Alexandria: The First Systematic Theologian

While Tertullian was forging a Latin theological vocabulary in Carthage, another African giant was pioneering a different, but equally influential, approach to Christian thought in the east. In the cosmopolitan city of Alexandria, a scholar of breathtaking brilliance and legendary devotion named Origen was working to synthesize Christian faith with the highest forms of Greek philosophy. If Tertullian gave the Western church its legal language, Origen gave the Eastern church its philosophical depth, establishing a legacy of intellectual rigor and spiritual interpretation that would echo for centuries.[20]

Born around 185 CE to a devout Christian family in Alexandria, Origen's life was marked from its earliest moments by intense intellectual and spiritual passion. His father, Leonides, was a respected teacher who personally instructed his son in the scriptures. When Leonides was martyred during the persecution of Emperor Septimius Severus in 202 CE, the teenage Origen was so eager to join his father in martyrdom that his mother had to hide his clothes to keep him at home. Thrown into poverty, the young prodigy began supporting his family by teaching grammar, but his reputation as a biblical scholar grew so quickly that by the age of eighteen, he was appointed head of the Catechetical School of Alexandria, the most important institution of Christian learning in the world.

Under Origen's leadership, the school became a veritable Christian university. He understood that to be credible in a city like Alexandria, Christian faith had to engage with the great philosophical questions of the day. He studied under the leading pagan philosophers of his time and mastered the art of Platonic and Stoic thought. But his goal was not simply to adopt these philosophies; it was to show that the deepest truths they hinted at were fully and perfectly revealed in the person of Jesus Christ and the words of scripture.

To do this, Origen developed a sophisticated method of biblical interpretation known as the allegorical method. He taught that scripture had three levels of meaning, corresponding to the human person's body, soul, and spirit. There was the literal, or "bodily," sense of the text; the moral, or "soulish," sense that applied to the life of the individual believer; and the spiritual, or "allegorical," sense that pointed to the profound mysteries of God and the cosmos. This approach allowed him to move beyond apparent contradictions or morally difficult passages in the Old Testament to uncover what he believed was their deeper, Christ-centered meaning. It was a revolutionary way of reading that allowed Christianity to be presented not as a collection of ancient stories, but as a comprehensive and intellectually satisfying worldview.

Origen's scholarly output was staggering. Ancient sources claim he wrote thousands of works, from detailed commentaries on nearly every book of the Bible to letters, sermons, and theological treatises. His most monumental achievement was the *Hexapla*, a massive work of textual criticism on the Old Testament. In it, he arranged six different versions of the biblical text—the original Hebrew, a Greek transliteration of the Hebrew, and four different Greek translations—in parallel columns. It was an act of scholarly devotion on a scale that would not be attempted again for over a thousand years, and it demonstrates the incredible intellectual resources available in Christian Alexandria.

His most famous work, however, is *On First Principles*, the first attempt in Christian history to create a complete and systematic theology. In this ambitious book, Origen laid out a comprehensive vision of reality, covering the nature of God, the pre-existence of souls, the freedom of the will, the fall from grace, and the ultimate restoration of all things in Christ. He argued that all intelligent beings—humans, angels, and even demons—were originally created as pure spirits, or "minds," who fell away from God through their own free will. History, he proposed, was a long, divine process of education and healing, designed to lead all souls back to union with God. "The end and consummation of the world," he wrote, "will take place when everyone shall be subjected to punishment for his sins; a time which God alone knows, when He will bestow on each one what he deserves."

Origen's thought was bold, speculative, and often controversial. His ideas about the pre-existence of souls and the eventual salvation of all beings (including the devil) were met with suspicion by some of his contemporaries and were later condemned by church councils. His life was also marked by conflict with church authorities, leading him to leave Alexandria and establish a new school in Caesarea in Palestine. He died in 254 CE from injuries sustained during the Decian persecution, having remained steadfast in his faith to the end.

Despite the controversies, Origen's influence is immeasurable. He was the first Christian thinker to create a truly comprehensive theological system, and he established the principle that Christian faith must be able to engage with the highest forms of human reason. His allegorical method of interpretation would dominate Christian biblical scholarship for centuries, and his deep and reverent engagement with the mysteries of the faith inspired generations of theologians. He stands as a towering testament to the intellectual power of African Christianity, a man whose mind was as vast and deep as the scriptures he dedicated his life to understanding.

Athanasius of Alexandria: The Champion of Orthodoxy

The theological fires stoked by Origen in Alexandria did not die with him; they blazed into the fourth century, illuminating the path for one of Christianity's most tenacious and consequential defenders: Athanasius of Alexandria. If Tertullian was the church's lawyer and Origen its philosopher, then Athanasius was its unyielding champion, a man whose entire life was a battle for the very heart of the Christian faith. Small in stature but colossal in spirit—his enemies derisively called him the "black dwarf"—this African bishop stood against the full might of the Roman Empire to defend the doctrine of Christ's divinity.

Born in Alexandria around the year 296 CE, Athanasius grew up in a city where the Christian faith was no longer a persecuted minority but a powerful, and increasingly fractious, public force. The air in the city crackled with theological debate, as competing schools of thought argued passionately in the marketplaces and lecture halls. As a young man, he became the protégé of Bishop Alexander of Alexandria, and it was as a deacon at his side that he first entered the great theological battle that would define his life: the Arian controversy.

The dispute began with a popular and charismatic Alexandrian priest named Arius, who taught that Jesus, the Son of God, was not eternal but had been created by the Father at a specific point in time. To Arius, the Son was a divine being, but a subordinate one. To Athanasius, this was not a minor theological disagreement; it was a catastrophic error that undermined the very possibility of salvation. If Jesus was merely a creature, however exalted, he could not bridge the infinite gap between humanity and God. Only God could save, and therefore, Jesus must be fully God.

The controversy grew so fierce that it threatened to split the church and destabilize the empire. In 325 CE, the Emperor Constantine convened the first great ecumenical council in Nicaea to settle the matter. The young deacon Athanasius, though not yet a bishop, attended with his mentor and played a crucial role in the proceedings. He argued with fierce conviction that the Son was *homoousios*—a Greek term meaning "of one substance"—with the Father. It was this concept, championed by Athanasius, that was enshrined in the Nicene Creed, which declared that Jesus was "God from God, Light from Light, true God from true God, begotten, not made, consubstantial with the Father."[21]

This victory at Nicaea, however, was only the beginning of Athanasius's struggle. The Arian party was powerful and had friends in high places. Shortly after becoming Bishop of Alexandria in 328 CE, Athanasius found himself the target of relentless political and theological attacks. Over the course of his nearly five-decade episcopacy, he would be exiled from his city no fewer than five times by four different Roman emperors, spending a total of seventeen years as a fugitive. He hid in the harsh Egyptian desert, sheltered by the monks who revered him, all the while writing letters and treatises to defend the Nicene faith. His motto became *Athanasius contra mundum*—"Athanasius against the world."

It was during these periods of trial that he wrote his theological masterpiece, *On the Incarnation*. In this profoundly beautiful work, he laid out the divine logic of salvation. He argued that human beings, created in God's image but fallen into sin and corruption, could only be restored by the Creator Himself. Therefore, God the Word had to become human to remake humanity in His image. It is here that he penned his most famous and influential line, a summary of the entire Christian vision of salvation: "He was made man that we might be made God." This concept, known as *theosis* or deification, was not about humans becoming divine by nature, but about partaking in the divine life through grace—a profoundly African understanding of salvation as transformative union.

Athanasius's life was a testament to African resilience. He was a man who understood the heat of the desert, the solitude of exile, and the unshakeable loyalty of the Egyptian monks who formed his personal army. His theology was not forged in a quiet study but in the crucible of conflict, persecution, and pastoral responsibility. His letters from exile reveal a leader of immense personal warmth and unbending principle, constantly encouraging his flock to hold fast to the truth. "The faith which you confess with the lips," he wrote, "keep in the heart inviolate."

In the end, Athanasius outlasted all his enemies. He returned to his beloved Alexandria for the final years of his life, his position secure and the Nicene faith triumphant. His life's work had ensured that the church would worship a Savior who was fully God and fully man, a doctrine that remains the cornerstone of orthodox Christianity to this day. He was the indomitable African champion who, against the world, saved the church from itself.

Key Latin & Greek Terms:

- **Homoousios** (Greek: "of one substance"): The key theological term from the Nicene Creed, championed by Athanasius, affirming that the Son shares the same divine essence as the Father.

- **Theosis** (Greek: "deification" or "divinization"): The concept, central to Athanasius's thought, that salvation consists of believers becoming, by grace, what God is by nature.

- **Athanasius contra mundum** (Latin: "Athanasius against the world"): A phrase that came to summarize his lonely and courageous stand for orthodoxy against powerful political and theological opposition.

The African Legacy: A Comparative Synthesis

To view Tertullian, Origen, Athanasius, and Augustine as merely four brilliant individuals scattered across a continent is to miss the essential truth of their collective legacy. They were not isolated stars but a brilliant constellation, and the light they cast was distinctly African. Their shared context—the vibrant, often volatile intellectual and political landscape of North Africa under Roman rule—was the necessary crucible that forged their world-changing theology. When viewed together, their work reveals a powerful and uniquely African style of Christian thought: passionate, intellectually rigorous, deeply engaged with scripture, and shaped by the ever-present reality of conflict.

While they all shared this African context, each man played a unique and vital "role" in the great drama of Christian thought, wielding a different intellectual "weapon" in service of the faith.

First came **Tertullian, the Lawyer**. Fighting from the pragmatic, Latin-speaking city of Carthage, his contribution was **language and logic**. He approached theology as a legal case to be won, using the sharp tools of Roman rhetoric and jurisprudence to build an unassailable defense of Christianity and to prosecute heresy with ruthless precision. He gave the Western church its doctrinal vocabulary.[22]

Next came **Origen, the Philosopher**. From the Greek-speaking intellectual hub of Alexandria, his contribution was **system and depth**. He met the challenge of Greek philosophy head-on, not by rejecting it, but by mastering it. He built a comprehensive theological framework, demonstrating that Christianity could answer the most profound questions of the pagan world.

A generation later, **Athanasius emerged as the Champion**. Also from Alexandria, his primary contribution was **conviction and courage.** He was not primarily a legalist or a philosopher but a spiritual warrior, a relentless advocate who defended the faith's central claim about Christ's divinity against all odds, including the combined power of his theological opponents and the Roman emperor himself.

Finally, **Augustine of Hippo** arrived as the Grand Synthesizer. His unparalleled contribution was **integration and introspection**. He masterfully wove together the legal precision of Tertullian, the philosophical depth of Origen, and the doctrinal passion of Athanasius into a comprehensive theological vision, all while adding a profound psychological and spiritual depth that was entirely his own.

Their shared African context was not incidental to these roles; it was essential. This was not the comfortable, established Christianity of a later Europe. This was a faith living under the constant pressure of a powerful empire, surrounded by a dizzying array of competing philosophies and ancient religions. This environment forced these African thinkers to be sharper, bolder, and more innovative. They could not take faith for granted; they had to define it, defend it, and demonstrate its intellectual superiority every single day. This is the "So What?" of their story: their African context—the blend of cultures, the specific intellectual challenges, and the history of Roman interaction—was the very forge in which the doctrines of orthodox Christianity were hammered into shape.

This context produced a legacy of theological continuity that is nothing short of breathtaking. It was **Tertullian's** legal vocabulary that first gave the church the language of the Trinity. It was **Origen's** systematic framework that first attempted to create a comprehensive Christian worldview. It was **Athanasius's** unyielding defense that enshrined the full divinity of Christ at the Council of Nicaea. And it was **Augustine's** towering intellect that took all these threads and wove them into the rich tapestry of orthodox Catholic and, later, Protestant belief. The Nicene Creed, the foundational statement of Christian faith, is an African document—built with African vocabulary, defended by an African champion, and given its deepest philosophical grounding by an African bishop.

Their collective work stands as a powerful testament to the African Christian soul, a legacy best summarized by their own immortal words. One can hear in their voices a powerful crescendo of faith, moving from defiance and struggle to intellectual wonder, from divine hope to intimate human longing.

From the heart of persecuted Carthage, Tertullian cries out with defiant courage:

> "The blood of the martyrs is the seed
> of the church."

From the great library of Alexandria, Origen responds with boundless intellectual curiosity:

> "Our minds, which are shut up in the
> prison of the body, desire to break
> forth and burst the bars of their enclo-
> sure, that they may be able to behold
> the light of truth."

From the deserts of exile, Athanasius answers with a proclamation of world-altering hope:

> "He was made man that we might be
> made God."

And finally, from his small study in Hippo, Augustine brings this grand symphony to its deeply personal conclusion:

> "Our hearts are restless until they rest
> in You."

These are not merely the words of four men. They are the voice of African Christianity itself, a voice that speaks of resilience, intellect, hope, and a profound, unquenchable thirst for God. They are a powerful reminder that for the first four hundred years of the church, its heart and its mind beat strongest not in Europe or Asia, but on the continent of Africa.

Chapter 4

Ethiopia: The First Christian Nation

The Land of Frankincense and Gold: An Introduction to Ancient Ethiopia

The story of how Ethiopia became the first great Christian nation begins, as so many great stories do, with a moment of shocking violence and improbable grace. The fourth-century historian Rufinus sets the scene on the treacherous waters of the Red Sea, where a philosopher named Meropius and his two young Syrian pupils, Frumentius and Aedesius, were returning from a voyage to India. Their journey ended in catastrophe. As Rufinus starkly records, "The barbarians fell upon the ship... and slaughtered all, together with Meropius himself." But in the aftermath of the massacre, a strange miracle occurred. Amidst the wreckage and the dead, the local tribesmen found the two boys, not cowering in fear, but sitting quietly "studying under a tree." This small act of civilized defiance in the face of barbarism was enough to have them spared. They were taken captive and, by a twist of fate that would alter the course of history, presented to the king of Aksum.[23]

The kingdom these boys entered was one of immense power and antiquity. To reach the capital, they would have traveled from the coast up into the cool, rugged highlands of the Ethiopian plateau, a land of sheer cliffs and fertile valleys. The air itself would have told the story of the kingdom's wealth, carrying the heady, sacred scent of frankincense and myrrh harvested from the gnarled trees of the lowlands. This was the source of Aksum's legendary fortune. At the bustling port of Adulis, the excavated ruins of which still lie on the Eritrean coast, the remains of stone warehouses and shattered Roman amphorae mutely testify to a thriving international trade. It was here that the treasures of Africa—gold, ivory, and precious incense—were loaded onto ships bound for the great markets of the Roman Empire, Persia, and India.

The wealth generated by this trade was on full display in the capital city of Aksum. A visitor would have been awestruck by the towering granite stelae, some soaring over twenty meters into the sky, their surfaces intricately carved to mimic the doors and windows of royal palaces. In the tombs of the Aksumite elite, archaeologists have unearthed exquisite artifacts that speak of a sophisticated and cosmopolitan culture: finely carved alabaster bowls and elegant incense burners, their designs showing the clear influence of artisans from across the Red Sea in South Arabia.

This cultural exchange was not limited to goods and artistic styles. The very ideology of Aksumite kingship was intertwined with the worship of gods shared with their South Arabian neighbors. The king's authority was divinely sanctioned by the fierce war god, Mahrem. On towering stone monuments, King Ezana and his predecessors declared their divine right to rule with the unambiguous title: "son of the unconquerable Mahrem." Their military victories were not their own; they were achieved "by the power of Mahrem." This belief was the bedrock of the state, a public declaration that the king was the chosen earthly agent of a powerful celestial deity.

This public faith was not just etched in stone; it was stamped in metal and passed from hand to hand every day in the marketplace. To understand the world Frumentius and Aedesius entered, one need only look at the coins minted in the early years of King Ezana's reign. On their face is the king's profile, his authority clear. He is flanked by two stalks of wheat, a symbol of the agricultural abundance he guarantees his people. And floating above his head is the most important symbol of all: the crescent and disk, the unmistakable emblem of the old pagan gods. This was the stamp of legitimacy, a daily reminder to every citizen that their king, their prosperity, and their kingdom were all under the protection of the celestial powers.

It was into this proud, ancient, and deeply religious African kingdom that the two young, shipwrecked Christians were brought. Here, amidst the towering symbols of pagan power and the constant hum of a global marketplace, they would have to find a way to survive. But survival was only the beginning. Unbeknownst to all, their quiet arrival would set in motion a chain of events that would see the crescent and disk vanish from the kingdom's coins, to be replaced by the sign of the cross, and a powerful African king renounce the god of his ancestors to embrace the faith of his captive servants.

The Shipwrecked Saint and the Converted King

The salt and blood of the Red Sea still clung to the two Syrian boys, Frumentius and Aedesius, as they were marched through the gates of Aksum. Behind them lay the wreckage of their ship and the memory of a massacre that had claimed their mentor and the entire crew. But as the historian Rufinus would later record, a strange fate had saved them. They had been discovered, not cowering in fear, but sitting quietly "under a tree, engaged in study." This small act of civilized defiance in the face of barbarism was enough to have them spared and "handed over to the ruler." Now, surrounded by the towering granite stelae of the royal city and the clamor of a language they did not understand, they were brought before the king—not as guests, but as captives, their future hanging by the thinnest of threads.

In the royal city of Aksum, with its bustling palaces and markets, the two Syrian boys found their lives spared. Their intelligence and education impressed the king, and they were given positions in the royal household. Aedesius was made the king's cupbearer, a position of intimate trust. Frumentius, the more astute and capable of the two, was appointed as the king's secretary and treasurer, eventually becoming the most powerful advisor at court. For years, the two Christians served the pagan king with integrity, all the while quietly seeking out the few Roman Christian merchants who passed through the kingdom, gathering with them for prayer and nurturing a small, hidden Christian community in the heart of the empire.

When the king died, his son, Ezana, was still an infant. The queen regent, recognizing Frumentius's wisdom and loyalty, implored him to stay and act as a tutor and co-regent for the young prince until he came of age. This was the pivotal moment. For the next decade, the most powerful man in the Aksumite kingdom was a devout Christian, and the future king was his devoted pupil. Frumentius used his influence not to seize power for himself, but to shape the heart and mind of the young Ezana, teaching him the principles of Christian governance, justice, and faith. In the quiet of the royal chambers, away from the watchful eyes of the court priests of Mahrem, a slow and profound conversion was taking place.

When Ezana finally ascended to the throne, the seeds planted by his tutor came to fruition. He made the momentous decision to embrace Christianity as his own faith, and by extension, the faith of his kingdom. But a royal conversion was not enough; a formal church needed to be established. Frumentius, his duty to the kingdom fulfilled, traveled to the great city of Alexandria to report on the momentous events in Aksum and to request that a bishop be sent to shepherd the new community.

In Alexandria, he came face-to-face with the great champion of ortho-doxy, Athanasius. Upon hearing Frumentius's incredible story, Athanasius declared that no one was better suited to lead the new church than the man who had planted it. As Rufinus recorded, Athanasius, in a council with his priests, proclaimed: "What other man shall we find in whom is the Spirit of God as in thee, who can accomplish these things?" He consecrated Frumentius as the first bishop of Ethiopia, bestowing upon him the title *Abba Salama*, or "Father of Peace." Frumentius then returned to Aksum, no longer as a royal advisor, but as the spiritual father of a new Christian nation, forever linking the church of Ethiopia to the theological heart of African Christianity in Egypt.[24]

Forging a Christian Kingdom: The Rise of the Ethiopian Orthodox Church

The conversion of King Ezana was not an end, but a beginning. The private faith of a monarch, nurtured by his Syrian tutor Frumentius, now had to become the public soul of a nation. This grand project began with a public and permanent declaration of the new royal faith. The most powerful evidence of this transformation is carved into stone and stamped onto metal. The monumental inscriptions and royal coinage of Ezana's reign provide a dramatic, real-time account of this religious revolution.[25]

Early in his reign, Ezana's inscriptions follow the traditional pagan for-mula. On a great stone tablet celebrating a military victory, he gives full credit to his ancestral gods, declaring: "By the power of the Lord of All, and by the power of heaven and earth... I, Ezana, son of the unconquerable Mahrem, king of Aksum... made war". The language is that of a confident pagan ruler, secure in the favor of his traditional deities. His early coins tell the same story, their metal faces stamped with the crescent and disk, the unmistakable emblem of the old celestial gods.

But later inscriptions reveal a stunning theological shift. After his conversion, the references to Mahrem and the other gods disappear entirely. On a later monument, Ezana attributes his success to a new, singular power, proclaiming: "By the power of the Lord of Heaven, Who in heaven and upon earth is mightier than everything that exists... By the power of the Lord of Heaven, Who has made me king... there is none who can resist me." The "Lord of Heaven" was the common term used by Christians to refer to the one God. This was a public renunciation of the old gods and a formal declaration of allegiance to the Christian faith, etched for eternity in stone.[26]

This same transformation is visible on the kingdom's currency. The pagan crescent and disk symbol is abruptly replaced by the Christian cross. For the first time in history, a major world power had placed the cross on its official coinage, a tangible symbol of the kingdom's new identity that would pass through the hands of every merchant and citizen. Some coins even bore the Greek inscription, "TOYTO APECH TH XWPA"—"May this please the country"—a public prayer that the new faith would bring blessing to the entire nation.

With the king's patronage established, a uniquely Ethiopian Orthodox Church began to take shape. A monumental effort was undertaken to translate the scriptures and the liturgy from Greek into the indigenous Semitic language of Ge'ez. This was a crucial step, allowing the Christian message to speak directly to the hearts of the people in their own sacred tongue.[27]

This new faith found its most fervent expression in the rugged, contemplative landscapes of the Ethiopian high plateau. Following the tradition of the desert fathers of Egypt, holy men sought solitude in the vast, silent expanses of the mountains. Monasteries began to sprout in remote, almost inaccessible places—carved into the sheer face of sandstone cliffs or nestled on lush, green mountain-tops. In these monastic settings, a unique blend of Christian asceticism and indigenous African spirituality was born.

In the late fifth century, the Ethiopian church was further strengthened by the arrival of the Nine Saints. These were missionaries fleeing persecution in the Byzantine Empire after the Council of Chalcedon. They found a welcome theological home in Ethiopia, which shared Alexandria's Miaphysite theology. The Nine Saints established a series of influential monasteries that became great centers of learning and evangelism, spreading the faith far beyond the capital. They solidified the church's structure, ordained a new generation of local priests, and, most importantly, undertook a massive project of translating the complete Bible and other Christian texts into Ge'ez, ensuring the church would have its own rich literary tradition.

The genius of Ethiopian Christianity was its ability to baptize indigenous traditions, weaving ancient rites into the new Christian calendar. The most spectacular example is the festival of Meskel, the Feast of the Finding of the True Cross. On the eve of the festival, communities across Ethiopia gather to build massive bonfires, or *Demera*. As the sun sets over the mountains, these great pyres are lit, their flames leaping into the night sky, while priests in vibrant vestments chant and dance. This tradition powerfully merges the Christian celebration of Empress Helena's discovery of the cross with a far more ancient, pre-Christian rite of lighting fires to welcome the changing of the seasons. It is a moment of pure syncretism, where the smoke of an old African tradition carries the prayers of a new Christian faith.

In this way, from the personal devotion of a king to the public festivals of his people, Christianity became more than the state religion of Ethiopia; it became its very soul. It was a faith that spoke in an African tongue, prayed in African mountains, and celebrated with an African heart, creating a resilient and deeply authentic Christian civilization that would endure for millennia.

A Faith Carved in Stone: Art, Architecture, and Identity

The new Christian faith of Aksum, now the official religion of the king, demanded more than just new buildings; it required a new soul, a new voice. It was Frumentius, the former captive turned bishop, who understood that for the faith to be truly Ethiopian, it had to speak an Ethiopian language. He championed the monumental task of translating the rich, complex Christian liturgy from Greek into the indigenous Ge'ez. This was a profound act of cultural immersion. In the churches rising across the highlands, the Eucharistic prayers, the scriptural readings, and the hymns were no longer foreign sounds but were woven into the poetic cadence of the local tongue, making the faith accessible and deeply personal for the Aksumite people.

But this transformation was not without turmoil. While the royal court officially embraced Christianity, a deep-seated tension simmered beneath the surface. The old ways died hard. Imagine the young King Ezana, his heart and mind captured by the teachings of Frumentius, now facing the formidable challenge of leading a nation steeped in centuries of pagan tradition. The priests of Mahrem, the ancient war god of his ancestors, would have seen this new faith as a direct threat to their power and the cosmic order of the kingdom. Conservative nobles, their own authority tied to the old rituals, would have whispered in the corridors of the palace, questioning this new god and his foreign-born bishop. Ezana's conversion was not just a spiritual journey; it was a political tightrope walk, a struggle to reconcile his personal conviction with the immense weight of his kingdom's past.

This internal conflict, this struggle against those who "opposed him," is etched directly into the stone monuments Ezana erected. On one of his great inscriptions, he no longer thanks Mahrem for his victories. Instead, he makes a bold and defiant declaration of his new allegiance, stating: "By the power of the Lord of Heaven, who has helped me... I have conquered." He continues, attributing his success not to his own strength, but to the divine power of the Christian God, making it clear that his reign is now under a new and higher authority. This was a public rebuke to the old order, a king declaring that his power no longer flowed from the traditional gods of Aksum.

While stone inscriptions made permanent pronouncements, the most dynamic evidence of this struggle was the currency itself. The shift in coinage from the pagan crescent and disk to the Christian cross was a daily referendum on the kingdom's changing soul. Each new coin minted with the cross was a small act of revolution, a tangible piece of the king's new policy that circulated through every market and village. For a merchant accepting payment, a soldier receiving his wages, or a farmer paying a tax, the feel of the cross on the cool metal was an undeniable symbol that a new power reigned in Aksum.

Alongside this public transformation, a uniquely Ethiopian Christian identity was being forged in art and literature. While the grand, mono-lithic churches of Lalibela would come centuries later, the foundations of a distinct Christian culture were being laid. This new identity found its ultimate expression in the powerful national epic, the *Kebra Nagast*, or *"The Glory of Kings"*. Compiled from older traditions, this text wove together the stories of the Queen of Sheba, King Solomon, and the Ark of the Covenant, creating a foundational myth that positioned Ethiopia as God's new chosen nation. This epic narrative gave the Ethiopian people a profound sense of their own sacred history, a confidence that their faith was not borrowed, but was a fulfillment of a divine destiny. It was a story born in Africa, for Africans, and it would sustain their unique Christian civilization for the next two thousand years.[28]

The Throne and the Altar: A Perilous Union

The conversion of King Ezana set Ethiopia on a unique historical trajectory, forging a Christian kingdom that would endure for nearly two millennia. Yet, to see this history as a peaceful, unbroken line of faith is to miss the fierce political tensions that have always simmered just beneath the surface. From its very inception, the Ethiopian Orthodox Tewahedo Church was inextricably linked to the monarchy. The king was not merely a secular ruler; he was the "Defender of the Faith," the protector of the church, and the heir to the sacred legacy of Solomon and the Ark of the Covenant. This fusion of throne and altar gave the kingdom immense spiritual authority and a powerful sense of national unity. But it also meant that theological disputes were political crises, and political rivalries often wore the mask of religious piety. When political and religious authority are intertwined, any challenge to one becomes a challenge to the other. This perilous union, while a source of great strength, was also the seed of future conflict.

A Faith Forged in Fire: The Wars of Ahmad Gragn

This delicate balance was shattered in the 16th century during the devastating wars with the Muslim Sultanate of Adal, led by the charismatic and ruthless Imam Ahmad ibn Ibrahim al-Ghazi, known in Ethiopian chronicles as Ahmad Gragn, or "the Left-Handed." This was not a simple border conflict; it was a religious war of annihilation. Imagine the terror as Gragn's forces, armed with superior Ottoman weaponry, swept through the Christian highlands with the explicit goal of destroying the church. The air, once scented with the holy frankincense of the liturgy, was now choked with the smoke of burning monasteries. Ancient manuscripts, containing centuries of theology and history, were put to the torch. As recorded in the *Futuh al-Habasha* ("The Conquest of Abyssinia"), his troops "burnt and looted for a period of about fifteen years, and almost completely destroyed the mediaeval heritage of Christian Ethiopia". The

Christian kingdom survived, but the trauma of the Gragn wars left deep scars. It created a siege mentality that would define the Ethiopian psyche for centuries, a profound sense that their Christian identity was under constant threat, solidifying the church's role as the ultimate bastion of national identity.[29]

The Crown's Shadow: Modern Political Struggles

This legacy of faith and fury has continued to play out in complex ways in the modern era. Successive Ethiopian regimes have understood the immense power of the church as a unifying symbol and have often sought to control or manipulate it to serve their political objectives. Under the imperial patronage of Haile Selassie, the church was officially "the established Church supported by the State," owning vast tracts of land and enjoying immense prestige. But this close relationship made it a target. The communist Derg regime, which overthrew the emperor in 1974, officially disestablished the church, nationalized its lands, and even secretly executed its patriarch, Abuna Tewophilos. In the decades since, the church has navigated a treacherous political landscape, at times co-opted by the state and at other times resisting it, leading to internal schisms and painful divisions that often mirror the ethnic and political fault lines of the nation itself.

The Resilient Survivor

To understand Ethiopian Christianity, then, is to understand this enduring paradox. It is a faith of breathtaking beauty and profound spiritual depth, a faith that has produced the rock-hewn wonders of Lalibela and a rich tradition of art and literature. But it is also a faith that has been forged in the crucible of political conflict, a faith that has had to fight for its very survival against enemies both external and internal. It is this history of faith and fury that makes the Ethiopian story so compelling. This unique Christian civilization, a solitary survivor, stands as a powerful testament to the fact that Christianity in Africa was not a fleeting colonial import, but a faith capable of creating enduring, complex, and profoundly human societies. However, Ethiopia was not the only Christian kingdom to flourish in this part of Africa. To its north, along the fertile banks of the Nile in what is now Sudan, another set of remarkable Christian kingdoms would rise and fall, leaving behind a legacy that is only now being rediscovered. Theirs is the story of the forgotten Christian kingdoms of Nubia.

Chapter 5

The Forgotten Kingdoms: Christianity in Nubia

The Confrontation: The Pupil-Smiters of Dongola

The answer came in 652 CE. A great Arab army, fresh from its victories in Egypt, marched south along the Nile, intent on adding Nubia to the rapidly expanding Caliphate. They laid siege to Dongola, the capital of Makuria. From the perspective of the Arab commander, this was to be a swift and simple conquest. But they had not reckoned with the legendary courage and skill of the Nubian warriors.

The Nubians were masters of the bow, and their archers rained down a storm of arrows upon the besieging army with terrifying accuracy. The Arab chronicles of the event record their shock and awe, calling the Nubians *rumat al-hadaq*, or "the pupil-smiters," because their arrows seemed to unerringly find the eyes of their enemies. The siege of Dongola turned into a bloody stalemate. The Arab forces, unable to breach the city's defenses and suffering heavy casualties, were forced to withdraw. Nubia had done what the mighty Persian and Byzantine empires could not: it had halted the seemingly unstoppable Arab advance.[30]

The failed siege led to one of the most unique and enduring treaties of the medieval world. Realizing that a military conquest would be too costly, the new rulers of Egypt negotiated a pact with the king of Makuria known as the Baqt. This was not a treaty of surrender. It was a trade and non-aggression pact that established a framework for centuries of complex coexistence. In the king's audience chamber, with Bishop Kyros at his right hand, the terms were agreed upon. The Nubians would provide an annual tribute of 360 high-quality slaves to the governor of Egypt. In return, the Muslims would supply Nubia with wheat, wine for the Eucharist, and fine textiles. The treaty secured Nubia's political independence and religious freedom for over six hundred years, transforming the kingdom from a frontline state into a stable, peaceful Christian citadel.[31]

The Golden Age

By the seventh century the Nubian kingdoms had not only survived the upheavals that swept the Mediterranean and the Nile after the fall of Rome and the rise of Islam, they had fashioned a striking, durable civilization of their own — a Christian Golden Age whose monuments, manuscripts and money tell a clear, concrete story.

At the heart of that story stand individual rulers whose names still echo in church lists and Arabic chronicles. Chief among them is King Merkurios — remembered in contemporary Coptic sources as "the New Constantine." Merkurios appears in the sources of the late sixth and early seventh centuries (fl. c. 620s–650s) as the sovereign who turned Makuria into a fortified, assertive Christian state. As the Muslim armies pushed into Egypt in the 640s, it was Merkurios who organized the defence of the Nile corridor. In a series of clashes in the 640s and 650s Makurian horsemen and archers repelled incursions from the east; the stubborn resistance of Merkurios's forces culminated in negotiation rather than conquest. The resulting diplomatic settlement — crystallized in the Baqt pact carried into force about 652 — guaranteed an uneasy peace between Muslim Egypt and Christian Nubia that would endure, with intervals, for centuries.

Merkurios's contemporaries likened his role as defender of the faith to that of Constantine; it is no accident that church calendars remembered him by that lofty sobriquet.

A later monarch, King Georgios, embodies how peaceful diplomacy and long reigns consolidated Nubian prosperity. Ruling for forty-seven years (roughly c. 720–767 in many reconstructions), Georgios transformed Makuria into a regional diplomatic hub. His court in Dongola hosted envoys from Alexandria, Abyssinia (the Christian realms south of the Sudan), and even from Byzantine and Arab traders. Georgios negotiated grain and gold exchanges with Egyptian merchants, mediated local disputes with Alodian magnates to the south, and used marriage alliances to cement ties: royal daughters were given in marriage to neighboring Christian houses; at the same time, noble brides arrived at Dongola accompanied by Byzantine liturgical objects and Byzantine craftsmen. The result was stability — decades in which building and bookmaking could flourish.

Those decades produced architecture that still arrests modern visitors and archaeologists. In Faras (ancient Pakhoras) and at Dongola, royal and episcopal patrons financed ambitious church building campaigns from the late seventh through the twelfth centuries. The great cathedral at Faras — a brick basilica with a wide nave, flanking aisles, and a semicircular apse — was rebuilt and richly decorated in the ninth and tenth centuries (excavated layers date to c. 800–1100). Its walls were covered with frescoes of saints and donors, painted in brilliant lapis blues and cinnabar reds, where bishops and kings appear side by side. Monasteries expanded in the desert valleys: communal cells clustered around refectories and chapels, libraries were fitted into upper storeys, and bell towers were added to call the faithful. Nubian masons mastered the use of fired brick and rubble masonry; they invented compact domes over square naves and carved stone capitals that mix Coptic vegetal motifs with African animal imagery. Faras's painted bishops, Dongola's carved doorways, and the stepped buttresses of Alodian churches are the material proof of a confident ecclesiastical architecture funded by royal coffers.[32]

Those coffers were heavy, and gold explains much of the Golden Age's capacity. Nubia had been a source of gold since Pharaonic times; in the medieval period gold working and mining in the Eastern Desert and in riverside placers around the third cataract remained important. From c. 600 through the eleventh century, kings levied taxes on mining and controlled the caravans. Gold dust and ingots moved north to Aswan and Alexandria and south to the Red Sea ports; in exchange Makuria imported linen, luxury textiles, and glassware. It was gold — taxed, pledged, and melted for coin and ornament — that paid for bishops' salaries, supported monasteries, ordered fresco programs, and paid ateliers of illuminators.

Those ateliers were prolific. Scriptoriums attached to cathedral complexes at Faras, Dongola and Qasr Ibrim produced illuminated Gospel books, lectionaries and theological treatises in multiple tongues. From the ninth to the fourteenth centuries, scribes copied texts in Old Nubian (the language now known as Nobiin, written in an adapted Coptic script), in Greek for liturgy and theology, and increasingly in Arabic as contacts with the Islamic world deepened. The manuscripts ranged from small Gospel lectionaries used in the liturgy to grand illuminated evangelaria whose pages bloom with crosses, geometric borders and portraits of the evangelists painted in gold leaf. Some codices show a hybrid iconography: Byzantine-style haloed figures rendered with Nubian physiognomy and local dress, underscoring the kingdom's position at a cultural crossroads. Excavations have unearthed palimpsests and marginal notes showing that scriptoriums were working copies, translations and commentary — a lively intellectual culture, not a static conservatism.[33]

This flourishing of art and letters was not merely devotional. Royal patronage extended to liturgical art that announced dynastic legitimacy: kings commissioned icons and murals that pictured themselves standing before the Virgin or the Cross, robes edged with gold thread, crowns depicted in brilliant pigment. Diplomatic marriages brought not only spouses but portable wealth and liturgical objects: Byzantine vestments, Ethiopian illuminated psalters, and Coptic reliquaries found their way into Nubian churches, where they were reworked and reinterpreted in the Nubian aesthetic.[34]

Taken together, these facts — the military skill and religious zeal of Merkurios the "New Constantine," the long, diplomatic reign of Georgios, the brick-and-fresco cathedrals of Faras and Dongola, the humming scriptoria that produced trilingual manuscripts, the gold that filled royal treasuries, the art that fused Byzantine, Coptic and African influences — produce a vivid picture. Medieval Nubia was no peripheral backwater. Between roughly the seventh and the twelfth centuries it was a Christian polity with kings who defended its borders, bishops who commissioned masterpieces, miners and merchants who paid for them, and scribes who recorded, copied and embellished a faith that was distinctly Nubian.

A Sunday at Faras Cathedral

The peace secured by the Baqt treaty ushered in a golden age for Christian Nubia. Sheltered from the turmoil of the outside world, the kingdom of Makuria flourished, developing a vibrant and unique Christian culture. To understand the soul of this kingdom, one must step out of the blinding desert sun and into the cool, dark interior of the great cathedral at Faras.

As your eyes adjust, the walls come alive with magnificent frescoes, a symphony of color and faith. Here are scenes from the Gospels, but they are populated with Nubian faces. A powerful, dark-skinned Virgin Mary, her eyes lined with kohl in the Nubian style, cradles the infant Jesus. A Nubian king, his brow adorned with a royal crown and a saint's halo, is depicted under the protection of Christ himself. Archangels with brightly colored wings stand guard, their faces serene and their authority absolute. This was not a borrowed art; it was a confident, local expression of the universal Christian story, a declaration that the saints and kings of Nubia had their own sacred place in the hierarchy of heaven.

The service begins. The air grows thick with the scent of incense as the bishop, clad in ornate vestments, leads a solemn procession to the altar. The ancient Greek words of the *Kyrie eleison* ("Lord, have mercy") echo through the space, a resonant link to the wider Christian world. But then the chanting shifts into the rhythms of Old Nubian, the language of the people, as the priest recites prayers from a hand-painted Euchologion, or prayer book. A deacon reads from a Gospel book written not in Greek or Coptic, but in the newly developed Old Nubian alphabet, its letters telling the familiar stories with a new, local voice. In the quiet scriptoriums of the monasteries that dotted the Nile valley, monks labored over this burgeoning literary tradition, composing not only translations but also original legal documents, letters, and stirring accounts of the lives of saints.

Art and Architecture: Windows into a Lost World

Stepping into a Nubian church, even as the millennia fall away, is to step into a theater where color and devotion perform against the desert light. The surviving sanctuaries of medieval Christian Nubia — most famously the cathedral at Faras — were not spare desert chapels but sumptuous, carefully conceived spaces where paint and stone worked together to make heaven feel present on earth. The walls still speak in a vocabulary at once familiar and utterly local: Christ in the apse, face framed by an aureole of color; bishops and martyrs in rows; kings clasping scepters and crowns beside angels. The effect is both Byzantine and unmistakably Nubian.

At Faras the frescoes arrest you first by their humanity. The great Christ Pantocrator — the omnipotent ruler of icons — occupies the apse with the frontal stillness of Eastern orthodoxy, but his features register the Nile valley: a broad, dignified face, full lips, strong nose and dark, luminous skin. He is painted into the grammar of Mediterranean Christian art, haloed and stern, yet the physiognomy and the ornament that surrounds him root him in Nubia. Around him, local saints appear not as distant foreign types but as royal figures: bishops and holy men are arrayed in embroidered tunics and jeweled collars, their poses borrowing from court portraiture as much as from ecclesiastical tradition. Many saints wear royal regalia — crowns, belted robes, jeweled collars — a visual language that enfolds sanctity and sovereignty in a single gesture.[35]

Nowhere is the marriage of church and court more striking than in the royal portraits. Across Nubia's painted walls kings are shown receiving crowns from the hands of Christ or a saint. The scene is intimate and political at once: Christ above, bestowing legitimacy; the monarch below, robed and poised, anointed into a sacred kingship. Queens appear frequently, too, not as sidelined patrons but as visible donors — sometimes shown holding models of the very churches they commissioned, sometimes depicted in devotional posture, hands raised in prayer. Their garments are detailed with patterns that evoke local textile traditions and courtly finery; the way they are painted — with care for individual expression and weight of presence — tells us that royal women were active, visually acknowledged participants in the religious life of the kingdom.

Architecturally, Nubian churches fused traditions with imaginative practicality. The plan language of basilicas and apses came from Byzantine models, but columns, capitals and decorative motifs show Egyptian and Coptic influences; the silhouette of the buildings — squat, massive and weathering the sun — has a distinct African logic. Local builders combined stone and mudbrick, laying robust stone foundations where the Nile's floods demanded it, and rising with mudbrick courses above. Timber was scarce in this treeless landscape, so vaulting and roofing techniques were adapted accordingly: corbelled arches and brick vaults — sometimes built without elaborate wooden centering — spanned naves and aisles, creating airy interiors that nevertheless retained thermal solidity.

Those interiors were calibrated to the desert. Thick walls acted as thermal regulators, soaking up heat by day and releasing it slowly at night. Windows are narrow and high, admitting shafts of light that picked out faces and halos painted on the plaster; doorways and porticos gave shade. Plastered walls were whitewashed to reflect glare and then worked with layered pigments to create zones of color that felt cool and intimate. The painted surfaces themselves were more than decoration — they were practical, too: pigments such as ochres, carbon blacks, and glassy blues held up unusually well in this dry environment, and the overall effect of polychrome walls was to turn the interior into a luminous chamber, an engineered refuge from the desert glare.

What makes Nubian painting particular is its visual grammar, an artful synthesis of African and Mediterranean idioms. Faces are rendered with a bold economy — strong planes, spare lines, large expressive eyes — set in compositions that borrow iconographic conventions from Byzantine and Coptic models. Motifs drawn from indigenous textile, beadwork and jewelry traditions animate the borders and vestments of saints and rulers. Where Byzantine icons aim for otherworldly aloofness, Nubian painters often allow warmth and local specificity to enter: a saint's face might be modeled in the same stylized way that Egyptian reliefs long used, but the elaboration of a king's collar or the patterning on a queen's mantle will honor local aesthetics. The result is a new vocabulary: Christian images that speak in an African accent, insisting on the local body and the local court as vehicles of the sacred.

These treasures came to light in an act of urgency and international cooperation. In the early 1960s the rising waters behind the new Aswan High Dam threatened to swallow vast reaches of the Nile Valley that had preserved millennia of human achievement. UNESCO launched a rescue campaign; teams from many countries converged on Nubia to salvage temples, tombs and churches before the inundation. At Faras a Polish mission led by Kazimierz Michałowski uncovered a cathedral whose plastered walls were painted in astonishing colors. Conservators carefully detached the painted plaster, rolled and crated it, and carried these fragile witnesses — some now in Khartoum, many in Warsaw — away from the new lake's edge. The dry desert that had preserved the paint for centuries had not kept the buildings safe from the politics of modern dam-building; the rescue itself became part of the story the art tells.

What these walls and buildings reveal is a culture of considerable sophistication. The images testify to an ecclesiastical apparatus with taste, resources and iconographic knowledge; they show royal courts savvy about visual propaganda and theology alike. The blended architectural forms argue for a community that conversed with Mediterranean Christianity while maintaining local building know-how. Above all, they reflect a people capable of making a cosmopolitan faith profoundly their own — a Christianity that looked to Byzantium for liturgical models but spoke in Nubian faces, garments and gestures.

Seen up close, the art and architecture of medieval Nubia refuse to be read as provincial offshoots. They are, instead, windows into a complex, connected society that invested stone and paint with its highest meanings. In the hush of a painted apse, with Christ's solemn, Nubian face looking down, one feels the lived conviction that in this fragile desert place, human hands had fashioned a durable dream of the divine.

The Fading of the Light

The end of Nubian Christianity was not a single moment of catastrophe but a long twilight, measured in generations rather than years. To tell it as an abrupt extinguishing is to miss how faith, architecture, language and daily life braided together and then slowly unraveled, rewove, and persisted in altered forms. The story is one of slow attrition and adaptation: churches turned into mosques, languages became layered one upon another, and Christian rituals were bent and absorbed into new communal rhythms.

Below, the contours of that slow change are laid out in time and in material detail so that the fade can be seen not as erasure but as transformation.

A brief timeline of transition

- 13th century: After centuries of relative parity and the long-standing Baqt arrangements with Egypt, Nubian kingdoms face increasing pressure from changing regional politics; contacts with the Mamluk Sultanate grow more fraught and intermittent.

- 14th century: Economic dislocation and political realignments intensify. Archaeological layers across central Nubia show overlapping Christian and Islamic features. Bilingual communities—speaking Old Nubian and Arabic—emerge in towns and oases.

- 1365: In Old Dongola, the construction of a mosque is archaeologically attested; this building stands as a clear material marker of a new public religious presence within a formerly Christian urban core.

- 14th–15th centuries: Church buildings are often reused rather than demolished; inscriptions and graffiti mix Old Nubian, Coptic-derived scripts and Arabic. Family genealogies and place names retain Christian references even as outward communal forms shift.

- Late 15th–16th centuries: The institutional Christian hierarchy—bishops, organized dioceses—has largely ceased to function in the ways recognized in earlier centuries; small pockets of Christian practice and memories survive among communities now defined increasingly by Islam.

Political and economic pressure: the long squeeze Several forces combined to make conversion a gradual, often pragmatic, course. Trade was central. For centuries Nubia occupied a strategic place on trans-Saharan and Nile caravan routes; changing routes in the later Middle Ages shifted economic gravity toward the Red Sea and the coastal trade dominated by Egypt and new maritime links. As caravans and taxes rerouted, towns that had depended on riverine and overland commerce found their incomes diminished. A community that once fed and supported a sizable clergy could less easily sustain bishops, monasteries and church maintenance.

Political pressure from the north also altered incentives. The rise of the Mamluk Sultanate in Egypt produced a more formidable neighbor; Mamluk policies toward the southern frontier were uneven—at times treaties were negotiated, at times raids and demands for tribute intensified. Where direct military pressure occurred, conversion could be accelerated; more commonly, the Mamluk presence meant shifting alliances, increased movement of peoples, and the diversion of tax and trade systems that tied local elites to Muslim centers of power. Over generations, elite families who sought favor or security with Egyptian authorities intermarried with incoming Arab groups and adopted Arabic as a language of administration and upward mobility; religious affiliation often followed these pragmatic alignments.

Intermarriage and social change were not instantaneous conversions but long processes. Arab pastoral groups moved into riverine margins and oases, and marriage into local families created households in which bilingualism—and with it, religious hybridity—became common. Children raised in such settings heard Christian prayers and Arabic invocations in the same home. This produced communities where outward markers of faith could change while inward practices remained syncretic for a long time.

Archaeological evidence for gradual change Archaeology is a patient witness to gradualism. Excavations, most notably at Old Dongola and other Nubian centers, have disclosed strata in which church floors and baptistries lie immediately beneath later mosque constructions. Rather than leveling a site and replacing it wholesale, builders frequently reused masonry, arranged older altars within new orientations, and smeared over Christian frescoes with new plaster. Radiocarbon dating and stratigraphy show continuity of occupation: households, workshops, and cemeteries continued to function even as their ritual centers were modified.

Material continuity shows up in ceramics, coins and household goods. Pottery styles slowly evolve rather than being abruptly replaced, implying that domestic life adapted at a pace different from official religious affiliation. Finds of coins from Egyptian mints alongside continued local ceramic types point to changed economic orientations without immediate social rupture. In cemeteries, one finds Christian-style burials adjacent to or even underlying Islamic ones; grave goods and burial orientation sometimes blend traditions—practices altered not overnight but in dialogue across generations.

Inscriptions and graffiti provide another line of evidence. Bilingual inscriptions—Old Nubian or Coptic phrases written near Arabic prayers—attest to communities operating in two scripts and two sacred vocabularies. Graffiti scratched by pilgrims and traders show overlapping names and saints; Arabic invocations placed alongside references to Christian saints indicate that popular piety often retained saints' cults even as official structures changed.

Persistence of Christian traditions: architecture, memory, and toponymy Buildings do not simply vanish. Churches became mosques or communal halls; architectural features—the basilica plan, column bases, carved capitals—remained visible and in use. In some converted edifices the mihrab was inserted into a nave; in others, the old sanctuary functioned as a sanctified space repurposed for new forms of prayer. These spatial continuities meant that people continued to meet in familiar places, and the loci of memory persisted.

Place names are especially durable. Villages, wells, and neighborhoods named for saints or Christian celebrations often kept those names long after the inhabitants had embraced Islam. Travelers and later local oral historians reported family memories of saintly founders, outbreak stories, and festivals that preserved Christian referents even when the outward rites assumed Islamic forms. In many cases, a shrine to a Muslim wali (local saint) may rest on a former Christian holy place, inheriting legends and pilgrimage patterns that once honored martyrs or bishops.

Specific examples of cultural continuity and adaptation

- Converted spaces: At several sites archaeologists have uncovered churches where liturgical niches and iconographic plaster remain beneath later Islamic additions. The structural memory of the church—its orientation, stonework, and ornament—left a visible imprint on later constructions.

- Bilingual inscriptions: Stones and ostraca show names in Old Nubian or Coptic alongside Arabic. These are not only administrative records but marks of identity; an Arabic tax receipt may sit beside a scratched invocation to a Christian saint.

- Household ritual: Ethnographic records from later centuries and folkloric traces show that house blessings, protective charms, and certain feast-day customs retained Christian forms repurposed within Muslim frameworks. Elements of baptismal symbolism, for example, can be detected in washing rituals connected to life-cycle events long after communal baptism ceased to be publicly administered by a bishop.

- Cemeteries and burial practices: Continuities in grave orientation, reuse of Christian tombstones, and overlapping burial grounds indicate a negotiated transition in funerary norms. In some places families continued to bury their dead in older Christian cemeteries even as they adopted Islamic prayer formulas.

The last echoes of organized Christianity

Institutional Christianity—the diocesan networks, the regular rhythms of bishoprics and monastic economies—was the first to fray. As funding, clerical recruitment and civic support dwindled, the formal offices that kept a widespread ecclesial life alive contracted. Remote monasteries, which had been centers of learning and ritual, persisted longer where geography insulated them, but many gradually fell into disrepair or were abandoned as younger generations sought security in towns aligned with Muslim trade and polity.

The traces left behind were not only stones but words. Family genealogies, local legends, place names and a scattering of documentary references preserve the memory of Christian structures into the 15th and sometimes 16th centuries. By then, the centralized institutions—church councils, episcopal appointments—had largely ceased to function in the organized way they had. What remained circulating in daily life were rituals, memories, and built forms that had been Christian in origin but adapted to a new world.

In the end, the "fading of the light" is better imagined as a slow dimming, with embers of practice and memory that glowed long after the main flame had altered its shape. Nubian Christianity did not vanish so much as migrate into language, stone and household habit—transformed, sometimes hidden, but visible to anyone who looks carefully at the palimpsest of walls, graves and names. That is the humbling lesson the ruins teach: cultural and religious change is often messy, protracted, and stubbornly local. It is in the folds of that messy history—where mosaics meet plaster, where Arabic script overlays Old Nubian prayers—that the real story of continuity and conversion can be read.

For centuries, the Christian kingdom of Makuria thrived, a peaceful and prosperous African citadel protected by its treaty and its faith. The churches were full, the monasteries were centers of learning, and its unique Christian culture was in full bloom. But no golden age lasts forever. From the 13th century onwards, a slow decline began. Internal dynastic disputes weakened the monarchy, and increased interference from the powerful Mamluk sultans in Egypt put the Baqt treaty under strain. The gradual migration of Arab tribes into Nubia began to slowly shift the demographic and religious balance of the region.

There was no single, catastrophic event that ended Christian Nubia. It was, instead, a slow fading of the light. The great cathedral at Faras, once the vibrant heart of the kingdom's faith, eventually fell into disuse, its magnificent frescoes slowly buried by the shifting desert sands. The Old Nubian language was replaced by Arabic, and the faith that had defined the river kingdoms for nearly a thousand years began to recede into memory. The story of this incredible African Christian civilization was largely forgotten, buried under the sand and lost to the history of the wider world, waiting for the spades of modern archaeologists to bring its glory back into the light.

Daily Life in Christian Dongola

Dawn in Dongola arrived first as a slow, silver widening on the great river. Before the sun climbed free of the eastern floodplain, the city's silhouette — mud-brick houses, clustered towers, and the rising forms of basilicas ringed with low chapels — was mirrored in the Nile. A small bronze bell somewhere in the cathedral compound began to toll, its clear note threading through alleys where laundry still steamed and embers from the night's hearths faintly smoked. The sound called people out: not in a single rush but in a measured, familiar unfolding of the day.

By market hour the riverside quarter had become a theater of color and clatter. Traders from upriver and beyond unrolled reed mats and placed their goods: pyramids of grain — sorghum and millet — baked flatbreads stacked like sun-browned lilies, clay jars and bowls whose pale glaze caught the morning light. Potters, hands dark with slip, beat and smoothed rims; a child perched near a wheel, her laughter higher than the bargaining that rose in Nubian, Coptic, and the occasional Arabic of visiting merchants. Gold, too, had its place: not the hoarded, imperial bullion of distant courts but the small, intricate work of local smiths — thin chains, delicate crosses, the fluted earrings favored by townswomen — all glinting like promises behind a woven screen. Nearby a stall perfumed the air with frankincense resin and powdered herbs, and the vendor, voice pitched low and persuasive, teased out how much of the sacred smoke a household might afford for a festival.

The market's smells were a map of Dongola itself: the yeasty tang of fresh bread, the dry dust of grain, the sweet and resinous bite of incense, and the river's briny breath. Men and women moved through it with the easy economies of long acquaintance. Deals were struck with a nod or with an exchange of small silver coins; gifts — a bowl of dates, a loaf — were given to a visiting priest as much for respect as for affection.

At home the rhythm of Christian life was woven into domestic routine. Houses were built around shaded courtyards, walls whitewashed and, where families had means, painted with simple Christian symbols — a cross, a fish, a small scene from a psalm. Morning prayers came with the first brightening, a few verses murmured over bowls of sorghum porridge steaming in clay. An oil lamp soothed the dark corner where icons were kept: carved wooden crosses with the distinctive hooked arms of Nubian artisans; glass-encased images brought from Egypt or painted by local hands in rich reds and ochres, their halos traced with gold leaf. Fathers, mothers, and children touched the surfaces gently, kissed them, and exchanged the brief liturgical blessings that tied household to church.

Children learned the contours of their faith in language that was their own. Old Nubian — the living tongue in which scripture passages, saints' lives, and homilies were being written and taught — flowed easily from teachers' mouths. In courtyards and in the shade of fig trees, small groups repeated Bible stories: David's courage, Mary's visit, the parables of Jesus. The tales were not academic recitations but the stuff of play: a boy reenacting a disciple, a girl gathering palm fronds to fashion makeshift crosses. Literacy was modest but growing; where a house could afford it, a child sat with a codex, tracing the angular characters that had been adapted from Greek and Coptic alphabets, learning to read the Word in their own script.

Domestic work had its own cadence: women ground grain with wooden querns, the repetitive creak serving as a kind of mnemonic for prayer; men repaired fishing nets or tended date palms; neighbours shared labor in threshing or in the heavier tasks of moving mud for a new wall before the dry season hardened the bricks. Food reflected the land and river — flatbreads, stews thick with sorghum, Nile fish slowly roasted over coals, sauces thickened with sesame, dates and figs for sweetness — and the spices of trade, the small luxury of imported pepper or preserved lemon on feast days.

Feasts and fasts stitched the weeks into a sacred cloth. Palm Sunday was a pageant of sound and scent: children waving palm fronds borrowed from the riverbank, townspeople forming a procession that wound from neighborhood chapels to the cathedral steps. Hymns rose in layered voices, sometimes in the liturgical Coptic tones, sometimes in Nubian cadences, the music a living hybrid that sounded both of Alexandria and of the Sahara. The air filled with crushed green leaves and the smoke of incense, and the procession halted for readings, for the blessing of palms, and for the communal anticipation of Holy Week.

Epiphany — the celebration of Christ's manifestation — turned the Nile into an altar. Early in the morning, the faithful gathered along the riverbank, priests in resplendent vestments carrying icons and the cross. A rite of water blessing took place, hands and crosses dipping into the current; water was drawn and splashed over brow and forehead, a sacramental mingling of Nile and prayer. The scene was not merely Byzantine pageantry transported whole: here the water rite bore the intimacy of a river that fed the city's body and soul, theologically meaningful and ecologically real. Onlookers lifted jars to be touched by blessed water, and children squealed as priests flicked droplets that caught the sun and made tiny, fleeting rainbows.

Easter in Dongola was an all-night conversazione of prayer and light. Churches were frescoed inside with saints and scenes whose pigments remained bright despite the desert dust — we still find traces of these paintings in the ruins — and during the vigil, torches and oil lamps threw those figures into a trembling new life. The liturgy moved through a long night of readings, psalms, and chants until the first triumphant cry announced the resurrection. People returned home bleary-eyed and exhilarated, bringing a quiet triumph into humble kitchens where the fast was broken with small cakes, sharp cheeses, and cups of sweetened tea.

Priests walked the city like threads through a tapestry, their movements setting tempo for both pious and secular routines. A bishop's sandals clacked on the paved causeways as he made his rounds; a deacon's small handbell might be heard summoning a house-bound elder to Communion. Church bells — sometimes handbells, sometimes larger castings — marked canonical hours, each toll a punctuation that reorganized the day: morning prayer, noon office, vespers before the sun fell. Monastic cells and parish houses hummed with their own quiet practices, and the voice of the church — from sermon to charity distributions of grain — was a steady civic presence.

Underlying all of this was a cultural synthesis visible in dress, in architecture, and in the liturgy. The domes and basilicas of Dongola bore features borrowed from Byzantine and Coptic patterns: broad naves, apses for the sanctuary, iconostasis-like partitions. Yet murals and carved stonework bore African faces and local motifs; liturgical melodies that came through Alexandria were sung in local modes. The clergy wore vestments stitched in the styles taught by Coptic and Byzantine influence but embroidered with patterns that echoed desert flora and Nile fish. The result was not imitation but adaptation — a Christianity that belonged to the people who lived its rhythms beside this river.

As dusk settled, Dongola did not withdraw into silence but into a softer, communal hush. Lamps glowed against mud walls, the heat of the day exhaled, and somewhere a late vendor called out the day's unsold wares. The smell of cooking blended with the faint sweetness of last evening's incense. Above, stars pricked a sky older than any church, as if watching these ordinary, holy lives continue in their steady, human devotion. In that small city on the Nile, faith and daily life were braided so tightly they were hard to separate; prayer rose in the market, scripture lived in the kitchen, and the city's heartbeat was measured by bells, by hymns, and by the soft, enduring sounds of people making home.

Chapter 6

Christians in Chains

The ship breathed like a living thing. Boards swelled, tightened, and spoke to one another through the night. Down between decks, where light was scarce and air ran thin, people learned to speak without using their tongues much at all. One foot tapped—a small sound on wet wood—and was answered by another. Someone hummed a single tone. A second voice fell in around it like a low harmony. The sound moved, not as a song yet, more like a thread that hands can hold in the dark. An older man tried words he did not remember fully—"He bringeth out of darkness and breaketh their bonds"—and the others answered with a breath, a murmur, a small "yes." Call and response, the old method of heart talking to heart, found new life in a place where stars could only be guessed at through seams in the planks. It was not the full ring shout that would later circle a brush arbor, but it was the seed of it—an invisible circle drawn by ankles, breath, and hope.[36]

There were no books to pass around. The only pages were closed eyes, where bits of psalms glowed like coals; the only ink was saliva and tears. What could be carried, memory chose to carry: names, proverbs, the rise and fall of women's choruses, the calendar of fasting and feasting, the rule that one voice calls and many answer. Drums were forbidden, so the body remembered how to drum: a forearm thumped lightly against a rib cage, a tongue clicked against teeth, a heel found the boards' sweet spot. Pain bent the spine forward; memory straightened it.

At night, between the crew's watches, teaching moved quietly from person to person. A man pressed his lips close to a boy's ear: "If you want to go fast, go alone. If you want to go far, go together." He drew a cross with his thumb in the boy's palm—a blessing that needed no writing system. A woman, shorn bald in a coastal fort, re-braided a neighbor's hair by touch, using patterns that had once marked kin and place. Where a lash had opened skin, someone mixed oil and whispered, "Joy comes in the morning." When a child stared without blinking, a grandmother tapped a steady rhythm near the child's feet and drew an old sign on their brow. Not everyone on board had been Christian; not every Christian had been free. But in the hold faith remembered how to live without paper, as it had survived drought, war, and the long patience of planting.

Contested Baptisms

Along the coast the forts stood hard against the horizon. Inside their walls small chapels offered shade and some kind of order: a whitewashed room, rough benches, a plank for an altar, a wooden cross hung above. Before ships sailed, catechists taught what they could in the time they had. Often, this meant repeating simple questions and answers in a language not everyone understood. "Who made you?" "God made me." The sounds were learned before the meanings landed. A priest poured water from a shell. Sometimes a bowed head agreed; sometimes a hand forced it lower. Registers filled with new names—António, Maria, João, Isabel. Officers on the quay argued over what this meant. Some believed baptism changed their responsibility to the people they had bought. Others treated the rite as a superstition that sealed a transaction.[37]

Not every baptism fit a single mold. A catechist, perhaps a man who grew up near São Salvador in Kongo, sat under the eaves at day's end. He gathered women and children and taught a creed—"I believe in God the Father"—one line at a time. Then he told stories that met people where they were: Joseph sold by his brothers, then raised up; Daniel thrown to lions, then saved; Elijah lifted by a whirlwind, leaving his cloak for another to wear. He measured his words to the sea: people about to go into water without bottom needed stories that promised God finds his people there. He drew the sign of the cross in the air—no empire could own it—and handed out rosaries tied from cord—no port could claim them. Near him, a grandmother sang a lullaby from home; the children rocked their legs to its rhythm. For a moment, two separate musics remembered each other.

Ship's surgeons kept cool, tidy journals. They recorded how many took sick, how many died, how many ate, how many were punished. Some noted, without comment, "psalms were sung," "devotions permitted," "humming heard at night." A few named a "Prince" as the leader of a "pious exercise," taking a name from a rumor of rank and writing it as if it could be verified. Their pens cut narrow grooves across paper. The people below cut deep grooves into the wood, where salt and sweat would remember long after ink faded.

The Bible Without a Bible

On open water, when storms rose fast, the hull screamed like a wild instrument. Ropes sang a high, frayed note. Crew shouted commands in a language that many below now flinched to hear. Humming stopped; prayers began. Voices used different names: Jesus learned in a fort chapel, Mary seen in a statue, a sky-father who needed no statue, spirits who watched the bend of a river or the gate of a market. Then a leader started a story, and the scattered devotions braided together. The same shape returned again and again: a people trapped, a sea ahead, a voice like thunder, a path where there had been no path. No one said "Exodus." It was enough to say, "When God speaks, water does not stay water."

On another night a woman told of a boy sold by his brothers, who learned a new house's ways, refused a powerful woman, suffered for his "no," and later used the house's grain to feed those who had harmed him. She did not say "Joseph," but she ended, "When the season changes, set something aside for your people." Someone slid a piece of hard bread toward a man who had given away his portion two nights running because he could not bear the smell of the barrel.

A child asked why lions sometimes do not eat their prey. An elder smiled in the dark: "Not all mouths close when they should." Others smiled because the truth in it was older than any one book. Daniel came aboard without leather binding; Joseph wore no coat; Exodus became a weather pattern to watch: winds, water, a way. If no one could write, the hold wrote for them: We were slaves there. We went through water. We did not drown.

What You Can Hold

Days blurred at sea, but traditions kept time when clocks did not. Fast days returned. A woman kept Lent quietly; no sailor noted it. An old man declined meat the day it came—scarce as it was—and said nothing about why. A boy who had received a proverb noticed, and tucked his extra piece into the hands of a man coughing so hard he could not eat.

Names taught, too. A man still answered to Kofi. When a deckhand tried "John," he held silence until a friend tapped his foot twice. That night the humming circle turned "John" into a story. The next day the man turned when called—not because the sailor owned him in that name, but because a song did. The language of command loosened. An older calling—for the people to answer together—began to retune the hold.

Belief took the shape of life. "I believe in God the Father" meant "We are not alone under these boards." "And in Jesus Christ his only Son" meant "He hears low voices in every tongue." "He descended into hell" meant "He has been in places like this." "He ascended" meant "He is not trapped," and "we will rise" meant, at first, "We will breathe again under trees." No one argued fine lines in doctrine. Everyone learned to share water.

Chapel at the Fort

Near the Bight of Benin and Cape Coast, little chapels did their work before ships cut into open ocean. A timber split by a carpenter's adze served as an altar. One candle flickered, tugged by salt wind and crowded breath. "What is your only comfort?" the catechist asked. "That I am not my own," answered a young man with bound wrists. The teacher had not planned that moment. He blessed him anyway, as if blessing could go further than his words.

A woman stared at a statue of a mother and child. She whispered the name that mother had at home, then whispered "Mary." She did not think she had betrayed anyone. She believed the world had widened to hold the name she trusted. Letters sent from castles argued over what was happening. Some called the baptisms rushed and dangerous; others celebrated fast additions to heaven's rolls. People who trusted older spirits tied on bracelets with both shells and small crosses, letting their traditions walk together for a while. Two economies of faith ran side by side—sometimes touching, sometimes blending, sometimes contradicting one another in ways that would take time to sort.

A surgeon wrote, "At dusk, the Blacks sang psalms in their manner." Another letter said, "They are like children, easily moved." A third scolded, "They invent responses we did not teach," as though invention itself were disobedience. A catechist who had grown up in Kongo knew better: children learn best when they choose the answer. He taught them to say "Our Father," and when one boy said "Our Fathers," he let it stand. Plural fathers made sense on a day when none of your own could be seen.

Plantation Sunday

Land did not end confinement. A field can be a ship if you cannot leave it. On some plantations Sunday reduced labor, and shirts were cleaner. A master who wanted reputation allowed a yard service. A minister read verses aimed at obedience. He chose psalms about God seeing evildoers. Some heard hope and took it. Others ate what nourished and let the rest pass. Faith learned to "eat the fish and spit the bones," because doing it openly meant trouble.

After dark, a second meeting formed where the big house could not hear. The same Bible was present, but stayed closed. A woman told a story: "A trickster climbed a tree for honey he had no right to." Children laughed—tricksters always do. Then she slid, without pausing, into a story of chariots chasing exhausted people and water obeying a voice no whip could command. Most children missed the seam. The adults did not. Story had slipped under the fence.

A preacher stood on a stump. No hand the master honored had ordained him. He moved while speaking because sermons back home were danced as well as spoken, and because the body finds words when it moves. "Joseph went down," he said. "Jesus went down." He let the words sit. "We are down." He traced an arc with one hand in the dim light, and a river seemed to hang in the motion. The sound that answered him started low—a moan that became a yes, a yes that hummed, a hum that rose toward a shout. From the yard's edge it might look like disorder. Within the circle it was breath.

Call and response became doctrine. "Who are we?" he asked. "God's," they answered. "Where are we?" "In Egypt," a woman said softly. "Where are we going?" "Home," said a boy who had never seen the place he named. "When?" "Soon." "How soon?" "When He says." Laughter rose. Laughter can be belief, too. The overseer thought time was being wasted. The people were making time.[38]

The Circle that Teaches

In a corner where shadows lay deepest, a circle formed. Feet tapped softly—quiet enough to pass as wind to someone on the porch. A palm slapped lightly against a skirt. A song began with one word drawn out—just enough syllables to breathe it. The circle moved left in small steps; it held its center and passed the lead from one to another. No drum was needed. Breath, hands, and courage carried the song.

Inside that ring, short lines thickened into life. "Go down, Moses" was more than history. It was instruction: go. "Steal away" was not only sneaking away in the night. It was a promise of invitation—Someone else wants you home. "Didn't my Lord deliver Daniel?" required only a nod to swell into hope. Rings make doctrine when paper is scarce.

An overseer, listening poorly, heard nothing of the music's scale—the minor keys that still remembered the sea, the West African tonalities turned toward sorrow and then hope. He did not see the Kongo cross—east to west, water to land, life to death to life again—drawn underfoot one step at a time. Some cannot see a map unless it is printed. This map was bodies and the low "amen" that means, "Say it again until it is true."[39]

Things that Hold Memory

People hid what would fit under a shirt or inside a fist. A little bag on a cord held a shell that meant protection, a tiny cross gotten at a fort, sometimes both tied together. A woman moved beads on a rosary the way her grandmother once counted lentils. A man kept a small book he could not read because the one who gave it had put a blessing hand on his head. Objects remember touch when minds are busy with survival. Later, thin booklets appeared with verses chosen to guide and to control—stitched into cloth covers, carried in pockets. Some called them "slave Bibles." People read them, and read between their lines. They had always read between lines. It was how they stayed alive.[40]

A boy scratched a cross in the dirt with his toe. He did not know the word a scholar would one day use for it. He knew that the air felt easier in his chest when he stepped over that line. He stepped across it into light, and across it again back into dark. Doorways can be drawn.

The River

Years later, in a river that did not know their names, a man and a boy stood up to their knees. The boy's owner watched from the bank, cane tapping a rhythm of impatience. "What do you believe?" asked the man in the water. The boy swallowed and spoke the words as shape and song before sense: "I believe in God the Father Almighty." The man nodded. "And in Jesus Christ his only Son." Another nod. "And in the Holy Ghost." Women on the bank hummed approval, not to rush him, but to steady him. The man leaned the boy back and under—long enough to wash, not so long that breath failed. When the boy came up he coughed and clung to the man's shoulders, then, surprisingly, laughed. Laughter belongs to baptism, too.

A woman waiting held out a cloth. A grandmother whispered a proverb into the boy's ear: a sentence outsiders would never file as a creed. That night, the circle formed in a clearing. The boy overstepped, stumbled, and found an elbow and a laugh holding him up. "Little by little," someone said. A voice started, "Guide my feet while I run this race," and the boy understood—deep, beneath words—that running can be prayer, and prayer can be a race, even when ankles still feel the memory of iron.

Storm Log

The worst storm came on a moonless night. Men on deck yelled; the ship pitched; a barrel broke loose and thundered; the hold heaved like a chest trying to breathe. Below, the circle did not form; people hung on to whatever would hold them. In the chaos, someone started, "He maketh the storm a calm," and another answered, "So that the waves thereof are still." The lines were ragged; the words not exact. That did not matter. The shape of the psalm stood. A woman who did not know the psalm hummed a steady note underneath. A child threw up, cried, and slept. In the morning the deck stank of fish and fear, but the ship lived, and so did those below. Not everyone. Enough to sing again.

The surgeon's journal for that week would later read: "Severe gale. Provisions spoiled. Two dead. General discouragement. Psalms sung by the Blacks in their manner." The line said everything and nothing. What the page could not hold was the way the humming held people in place; the way the small yes became a gathered yes; the way the gathered yes taught the body to resist despair.

The Long Walk on Land

Not every ship landed at the same port; not every path to a field was the same. Some were marched in chains past chapels and counting houses; some were sold and resold in town squares; some were driven past churches with open doors that did not open for them. The circle of call and response moved with them. A woman taught a child to answer "God is near" when she said "Where are you?" A man taught a younger man to say "Soon" when he asked "When?" The answers were not escape plans. They were scaffolding, poles to hold a mind upright when everything else pushed it down.

In some places the Sunday yard service used a printed sermon and a hymn sung from a book. In others, no service was allowed. People sang anyway—quietly, in kitchens and cabins and fields. "Steal Away" was a plan sometimes. It was a prayer always. A watchman at the edge of a clearing tapped a rock three times if a rider approached. The circle's steps slowed. The leader made the lines short as breath. The ring held its shape until quiet returned. Then it began to move again.

Laying Hands

Illness came with work and with living close, and there were not enough doctors to go around, and not many who would come when called. In that vacuum, hands did what they had always done when a body ached: they laid on a shoulder, on a forehead, on a scar. Prayers were short, simple, and to the point. "Heal." "Help." "Guide." "Hold." People told stories of healings like they told stories of storms survived. The stories were not proof to a court; they were food to a community. "She rose after we prayed," someone said, and that sentence became a way to keep praying next time.

Women kept the prayers and the plans. They pinned cloths to mark a home where the sick lay. They taught children to carry broths and to sit still beside a bed. They led early-morning bands that prayed through a list of names—two for healing, one for work, one for a husband far away, one for strength to endure what could not be changed, one for courage to change what could. If anyone in the meeting doubted, they were not scolded; they were held in the circle until belief warmed again.

The Afterword of the Hold

The first circle lived in the smell of brine, iron, and bruised bodies. The second circle lived in pine sap and dust, with sounds of cows lowing and kettles knocking. Between the two were forts and chapels, catechisms and sermons, some forced, some chosen. Hands learned to say "Our Father" and "Our Fathers" in the same breath. Faith did not wait for a building. It sang with no drums. It prayed without candles. It baptized in a river that belonged to no one but God.

Books would come later, and congregational minutes, and covenants, and hymnals and newspapers and schools. Before all of that, a heel tapped wood. The first Atlantic theology was made there, in that small sound, multiplied, then answered. It could not be footnoted easily. It did not need to be. It saved what paper could not hold when pages were torn, or not offered. It said, "Say it again, and we will make it true." It said, "We were slaves there." It said, "We went through water." It said, "We were not drowned."

Chapter 7

The Invisible Church

Yard School: Catechism Under Watch

The questions came first, clipped and careful, the way lessons do when a watcher stands in the doorway. "Who made you?" "God made me." "What does God require?" "Obedience." Words landed as shapes of sound before they settled into meaning. The catechist kept his face plain, the children kept their hands still, and the driver leaned his shoulder to the post as if bored. Out beyond the neat lines of call and answer, a small thing happened and no one stopped it: a child said "Our Fathers, who art in heaven," and a ripple of quiet approval ran the edges of the yard. Plural felt right. In the space between the official lesson and the gathered hearts, the people found a way to hold the truth broader than the page could carry.

At night the book closed and the room opened. A leader lifted a short line—"Go down, Moses"—and the room replied like a tide. "Didn't my Lord deliver Daniel?" was less a question than a shared memory turned forward. "Wade in the water" did not explain; it instructed. Here, doctrine was not a paragraph but a practice. Meaning arrived in the reply, gathered in breath, carried in the body. Exodus became marching orders. Joseph became endurance and wise provision. Acts became the Spirit spread out among ordinary people. The yard's catechism was not discarded; it was completed, turned inside out by a people who knew how to answer.[41]

On feast days a banner came out and a street turned into a sanctuary. Saint Anthony for lost things and lost people; the Virgin for mercy; Saint James for long roads and hard labor. A rosary rattled against a palm used to rope and hoe. A vow made at the statue reappeared as a pot left on a neighbor's step. Beside these names, older guardians stood unshaken: a river spirit under a footbridge, an ancestor at a hearth, a sign traced with a shell and tied to a wrist with a charm. No one thought this was confusion; it was the sort of careful blending that keeps breath in a body. If a priest scolded, the song continued anyway—less in rebellion than in recognition of what had carried them this far.

On the last night of the year the room filled with breath and candlelight. Watch night began with testimonies too short to argue with. "I was kept." "We prayed; she rose." The preacher stitched a familiar thread through the hour—a boy sold and raised, a Savior who went down and rose, a people pressed down but not finished. When he called the room forward, it was not only about heaven; it was a public choosing to live by the readings they had made together—deliverance for the bound, courage for those in the fire, a God who hears low voices and answers in time. A line in sand became a covenant in the throat.

Printed words arrived with their own logic. Tracts urged quiet virtue. Plantation sermons chose verses about servants and masters. Even trimmed "Bibles" appeared—pages arranged to teach patience without promise. The people listened, then went home and told the same texts back to each other with the missing endings restored. A line from Daniel grew teeth again. A psalm found its edge. A teacher stitched a small catechism by hand, asking the old questions in a new key: "What is your comfort?" "That we are not our own—and that God has not forgotten us." Counter-text did not need a printing press. It needed a table, a voice, and a people ready to answer.

Most of the deep instruction happened over work. A mother set dough to rise and asked a child to say a line of the creed; she sealed it with a proverb: "God's bread takes time." A grandmother taught Joseph's story as both warning and wisdom: keep your body, keep your wits, keep a little grain for those who will need it. Before sunrise, a prayer band circled names, one by one: fever lifted, job found, cousin spared, courage given. The reports came back the next week in simple sentences that set expectation: "We asked; He helped." No argument could unteach what the room had seen. The mothers' board tested and received candidates with questions as direct as weather: "Do you know the Lord?" "Can you forgive?" "Will you come when we call?" When the day came, they walked them to the water.

This is how the yard's short answers grew deep roots: under watch and within whisper, in songs that carried memory, in processions that fed the poor as well as the soul, in nights that turned a page into a promise, in printed lines corrected by living mouths, in kitchens where creed and proverb braided, in circles where prayer became practice. The catechism did not disappear. It was turned inside out and worn, every day, until it fit. In the next chapter the same voice that learned to answer in yards and kitchens will raise beams, hang doors, and build rooms strong enough to hold the faith it has already made..

Songs as Scripture: The People's Commentary

The book closed at dusk, but Scripture didn't. It moved to the mouth and the body. A leader lifted one short line—"Go down, Moses"—and the room replied, not as echo, but as decision. In that back-and-forth, meaning thickened. The call set the frame; the answer chose how to live inside it. Doctrine wasn't argued; it was felt, weighed, and agreed upon in the reply.

Spirituals carried whole stories in a handful of words. Exodus was not a past event; it was a present map. "Go down, Moses" said that bondage can be named out loud, that Pharaohs fall, and that crossing water is a work God still does. Sung slow, the line was courage for another day in the field. Sung faster, with feet moving and shoulders lifting, it became marching orders: go, speak, lead, move.

Daniel stood beside Exodus as the theology of survival. "Didn't my Lord deliver Daniel?" was less a question than a verdict. Lions' mouths can close. Fires can spare. The refrain returned like a legal seal at the end of each verse—case closed, hope warranted. In the circle, the word "deliver" gained muscle: deliver from terror at night, from a master's temper, from the despair that says "nothing changes." Each time the room answered—"and why not every man?"—the scope of salvation widened from Bible hero to neighbor, from famous names to names on the prayer list.

Acts breathed in the water. "Wade in the water" taught that danger requires movement, not stillness; that signs appear if eyes are trained to watch; that healing and guidance meet people in motion. The song's short commands—wade, watch, see—turned listeners into actors in their own reading of Scripture. Where the yard had trained memory by question-and-answer, the night trained courage by step-and-answer: take a step; hear the room say "yes"; take another.

This is how call-and-response became a school. The leader offered a line like a thesis; the people tested it with breath and bodies. If the line rang true, the reply rose warm and unanimous; if it did not, the answer fell thin and the leader found another thread. Over time, a canon of lived texts formed—songs that always brought the room together because they always told the truth. In those songs, Exodus taught deliverance with a verb; Daniel taught endurance with a promise; Acts taught Spirit-power with a path through trouble.[42]

Performance was interpretation. A slow "Go down, Moses" turned into lament—truth told in a low key to keep the heart from cracking. A driving "Go down, Moses" shifted to command—truth shouted to keep the feet from stopping. A soft "Didn't my Lord deliver Daniel?" became memory—proof whispered to those on the edge of quitting. A loud one became summons—evidence held up to a God who had done it before. "Wade in the water" could be counsel for secrecy or a cue for courage, depending on tempo, leader, and hour. The same words, sung in a different key, made a new sermon without changing a line.

The circle made critics unnecessary. If a verse dragged the room toward despair, a testimony cut in—"He kept me"—and the singer adjusted. If a line felt too easy for a hard week, a mother's voice dropped the harmony darker, and the leader matched her weight. The community guarded its doctrine with the simplest tools it owned: pitch, pace, and reply. Nothing passed that did not help someone stand up straighter the next morning.

This is why the songs lasted: they told the Bible forward. They did not only remember that a sea once parted; they prepared people to look for a crossing. They did not only admire Daniel's courage; they trained mouths to say "He will deliver" when fear tightened the chest. They did not only celebrate miracles in Acts; they taught hands to move and eyes to watch for signals when the hour to move arrived. In rooms where paper was scarce, Scripture stayed abundant because the people agreed, out loud, to keep it so.

Saints, Spirits, and Syncretism

On feast days, the street became a sanctuary. A banner lifted in the morning light; candles flickered in cupped hands; a small drumline of footfalls kept time on stone. Black confraternities—lay brotherhoods formed by people who needed one another as much as they needed the liturgy—moved in solemn joy through neighborhoods in Brazil and Cuba. Their purposes were plain and practical: honor a saint, keep a vow, feed the hungry, bury the dead, pay a widow's rent, ransom a brother from a debt, teach a child prayers and letters. Devotion and mutual aid walked side by side.

Each saint answered an ache close to the ground. Saint Anthony belonged to lost things and lost people—keys, papers, children, hopes—and to the work of finding, which most days felt like starting over. Mary, mother most merciful, met motherhood's labor and loss with a face that could listen all day and not grow tired. Saint James—pilgrim and fighter—stood for the long road and the hard hill, for calluses, for blisters, for getting up again. In chapel and alley, these names kept the week steady: a petition at dawn, a vow kept at dusk, a pot of beans dropped at a neighbor's door because a promise is a promise.

Beside these names, older guardians kept their posts. A cross traced at the threshold marked a boundary no magistrate could redraw; a shell tied to a wrist remembered river power; a small bag under a shirt held what the heart trusted—seed, salt, a bead, a bit of cloth from a mother's headscarf. Underfoot, the Kongo cross—life to death to life again—was walked without a word: east to west in morning errands, west to east returning home by dusk. Steps made a cosmogram where chalk could not. The world, like the dance, turned and returned.

And the logic of the orisa—the ordered, relational map of power from Yoruba and Ewe lands—stood quietly beside hagiography. Where a saint held a virtue, an orisa held a domain; where the litany named intercession, the shrine named relationship and exchange. The people did not set them against each other so much as put them to work. A vow before Saint Anthony could carry a river's memory; a candle lit for Mary could receive a grandmother's proverb; a drumless procession could walk to a heartbeat taught long before baptism. The point was not to blend until nothing was distinct. It was to carry what saved—memory, power, mercy—forward without dropping any of it.

There were tensions. A priest might warn against "mixture," a catechist might scold a charm, a neighbor might shake a head at a procession that lingered too long at the corner shrine. But in the kitchen after Mass, a rosary lay beside a gourd; at the feast table after vespers, a hymn verse answered a proverb; in the courtyard after the procession, a child learned the Hail Mary and a hand-game song in the same hour—and no one thought the child was worse for it. Where life was hard, people took help in all the ways they knew God to be near.

Processions taught the city how the people prayed. A banner of Saint James drew men who worked with their backs; a Marian day drew women who carried households on their shoulders; an Anthony vow-day drew searchers of all kinds—the recently arrived, the recently bereaved, the recently forgiven. Each feast braided the week into a rope. Funds collected for candles paid for medicine. A guild formed around a saint's altar became a credit line for a funeral, a school desk, a patch of land. Devotion put food on tables because it put hands together—first in prayer, then in work.

Inside the chapel, the statue's painted eyes watched as a brotherhood called out names: a mother in labor, a sailor overdue, a boy in trouble, a sister who needed a trade. Outside, chalk marks and foot patterns sanctified the threshold and the path. The same people who kissed a wooden foot and pressed their foreheads to a blue mantle would step over a line scribed in dust that meant "crossing, protection, return." They did not see blasphemy there. They saw completeness: the saint's intercession and the ancestor's wisdom doing the same work.

If someone demanded a clean answer—Which do you trust?—the people had one: the God who hears low voices. Saints were friends of that God, strong in mercy. Spirits were creatures of that God's world, strong in place. A cross drawn underfoot called that God's order to mind; a rosary counted that God's patience one bead at a time. In the end, the test was simple. Did the rite keep a neighbor from despair? Did it raise a widow's head? Did it remind a boy he was more than his labor? If yes, keep it. If not, change the song, change the path, change the prayer.

So the year turned on feast-days that were also pay-it-forward days, on processions that were also headcounts for who needed help, on vows that funded small hospitals of food and friendship. In the spaces between altar and threshold, the people learned to live with complement and tension. The banner and the bead walked together. The litany and the proverb took turns leading. The city tried to sort them; the people refused to be sorted thinner than they were. They had crossed too much water to travel light in the soul.

Watch Night and the Altar Call

The year's last night drew people the way a lamp draws breath. Candles set the room in warm circles; the stove ticked; the benches filled with coats, shawls, and the soft rustle of paper fans kept for habit more than heat. Watch night began the same way each time: short testimonies, spoken plain. "I was kept." "We prayed; she rose." "He spared us in the storm." No one argued a testimony. It was not a point to win, but a witness laid on the table so others could eat. After the circle of thanks came confession—quiet lines about tempers lost, debts unpaid, reconciliations left until morning—and a prayer said by all for clean hands and steady feet. Toward midnight, the covenant was read aloud. Heads bowed, hands lifted, the room answered each line with a soft "Amen," not as punctuation but as promise: we will keep this, together, when the year turns.

When the preacher stood, he did not bring something the room did not know. He brought threads the room had carried all year—Joseph's long descent; a sea that must move; a Spirit that meets people in motion—and stitched them into the hour. "The boy went down," he said, and paused until the room breathed with him. "He learned a house not his own, kept his body, kept his wisdom, kept his hope; and in time God raised him to feed the same mouths that had harmed him." The Middle Passage fit inside that sentence without being named. "Our Savior went down," he said, "further than any of us; and God raised Him." The room answered in a tone too low to write: a hum with weight, the sound hope makes when it remembers its own history. "We are down," he said, "and not alone." He lifted a hand in a crescent, small as a wrist turning, and a river seemed to hang in the gesture. "We will cross," he said, and no one laughed at how far the water might be.

This was stump preaching even when the pulpit was a proper one: plain, pictured, paced to the feet as much as to the ear. The lines were short enough to be owned by those who would repeat them later at a table or a bedside. The stories did not shrink the people's pain; they yoked it to older pain and to older deliverance so the present could borrow courage. A sermon like that did not end at the benediction. It traveled in pockets and under tongues, ready to be taken out midweek when a word was needed to hold the body upright.

When the call came, it did not ask for the curious but for the convinced—convinced enough to stand up and be counted. "If this is your reading of God's Word—deliverance for the bound, courage in the fire, a path through water—come." This was not a private decision. It was a public yes to a people's shared interpretation. Feet moved down the aisle, some quickly, some as if pushing through mud, some carried by others' hands. Elders met them with quiet questions—"Do you forgive?" "Can you be forgiven?" "Will you walk with us?"—the kind that turn emotion into promise. A deacon's hand rested on a shoulder; a mother's hand found a hand; the room's low "amen" wrapped the front like a shawl.

The altar call was democracy in its holiest clothes. It called the room to decide again—not only for heaven, but for the way they would read and live Scripture together. It set the year's course in one gathered breath. A watch night without an altar call could end in sentiment; a watch night with one ended in covenant. When the clock reached midnight, there was usually silence—thick, listening, full. Then the room exhaled. Someone started a soft doxology; someone else a shout. People embraced, wiped faces, and laughed the way people do when a heavy load has been put down, if only for a moment.[43]

Before the lights were lowered, ushers carried the covenant list to the front table. Names had been added in careful script; some had been crossed out with tears. The preacher folded the paper, slid it into the big Bible, and laid his hand on the cover as if holding the year steady by touch. Outside, frost held the grass in a thin silver. Inside, the benches were warm where bodies had been. The doors opened to a colder air and a harder week, but the people stepped into both with a sentence fixed in their mouths: "He kept us." That line would be enough until Sunday—and then Sunday would add another line, and another, until the year was full.

Print, Control, and Counter-Text

The printed page arrived with an agenda. Mission tracts praised meekness, thrift, punctuality. Plantation homilies chose safe passages—"servants, obey"—and skipped the ones that might stiffen a back. Even "Bibles" appeared with careful omissions, pages trimmed to teach patience without promise, counsel without confrontation. On Sunday mornings, words came down the aisle bound in leather and certainty. They were meant to curb the tongue, steady the hands, and keep hope within authorized borders.

But the page did not have the last word. The people read what they were given—and then read it back to each other, corrected. A sermon about obedience returned to the cabin as a story about Joseph's wisdom and Daniel's courage. A printed moral—"be content"—picked up a whispered ending: "until God says move." The practice became second nature: hear a line, test it against the whole story, adjust the ending, keep what feeds, leave what starves. Counter-reading did not need a library. It needed a circle and the habit of answering aloud.

Even where paper was scarce, margins filled up. In hymn leaflets and hand-me-down catechisms, small hands penciled helps: a gloss above "jailer" ("like the man with the keys"), a star by "deliver" ("He still does"), a cross beside "water" ("see wade"). Where writing was forbidden, memory kept the notes—an extra refrain here, a changed verb there, a pause that let the room breathe before a hard line. Selective memory was not carelessness; it was conscience. Refusal had forms, too: a verse skipped, a printed moral left unsung, a plantation text left in the pew in favor of a spiritual the room trusted more.

In time, new pages appeared from familiar hands. A schoolmaster with rough knuckles stitched a chapbook: the Lord's Prayer, the Ten Commandments, the Beatitudes, and three psalms that had kept his mother alive. A lay exhorter copied sermons in tidy script, pared to lines short enough to preach from a stump and strong enough to travel in a pocket. A choir leader gathered hymn texts—spirituals alongside Watts and Wesley—arranged by season and need: sorrow, endurance, healing, victory, watch-night. A mother wrote a primer for "the little ones": a letter a day, each with a verse and a proverb, so that "A" taught "Ask," "B" taught "Bread," and "C" taught "Comfort."

These homegrown texts did not shout. They fit a palm, a pocket, the space between a ledger and a lunch pail. They bore the marks of kitchen tables: flour in the crease, lamp-smoke at the corner, a child's drawing in the back. They also bore a method. Questions stayed—"Who made you?"—but the answers grew: "God, who made us free," "God, who delivers," "God, who sees." Where the official catechism stopped at "duty," the local one added "neighbor," "widow," "stranger," "enemy." Where plantation homilies flattened Acts into manners, chapbooks restored its movement: pray, listen, go, help, come back and tell.

Print could control from a distance, but it could not hold a room already trained in call-and-response. If a tract pressed too hard toward quietism, a testimony lifted it back toward courage. If a curated Bible clipped the prophets, a grandmother supplied the lines by heart. If a plantation text quoted Ephesians, a deacon answered with Exodus—and the room chose which to stand on this week. The page had authority; the people had discernment. Between them, a counter-text took shape—not a rebellion for its own sake, but a reading truer to the God who had met them in storms and circles and rivers.

By the time independent congregations printed their minutes and covenants, the habit was set. New hymnals bound the old spirituals to Wesley's lines without apology. Discipline manuals kept rules of reconciliation beside promises of mercy. Newspapers announced revivals, ordinations, and school drives; in the same columns, they published letters from lay teachers swapping lessons and memory aids. The people who had learned to sing the Bible wrote it down in their own hand—not to replace the Great Book, but to speak with it in the voice they had forged: plain, patient, courageous, and free.

Women Catechists and Prayer Bands

The best school in town was a kitchen table. A mother set dough to rise and set a child to recite. "I believe in God the Father." "Say it again, and slower." When the line held steady, she sealed it with a proverb: "God's bread takes time." The creed came one clause at a time, braided with lullabies and stories that fit the day's needs. Joseph's "no" taught a girl how to guard her body and her name. Hannah's long prayer taught a boy that tears do not disqualify faith. A psalm hummed over a fevered forehead taught a room that God hears whispers just as surely as shouts. By the time night fell, the children had carried half a catechism in their mouths, and none of them had seen a book.

Prayer bands met before the sun decided the color of the sky. Three or five or seven gathered, not to talk long but to agree quickly. The list lay simple: a neighbor's cough, a son at the river, a husband between jobs, a girl whose spirit had grown thin, a case in court, a field that needed rain, a field that needed rest. One short psalm—lined out for those who needed it. One verse from a hymn that could be sung with eyes closed. Then names, each name wrapped in a single verb: heal, keep, guide, deliver, steady. They did not argue doctrine; they proved it. Reports returned week by week: "She rose." "He found work." "The judge listened." Where answers delayed, they kept the names on the list and added "strength" so waiting did not destroy belief. In those circles, healing, providence, and guidance were not themes. They were muscle memory—practiced until they felt as ordinary as breath.

In the afternoon, the same women taught again—this time with hands. They sorted food into baskets, folded white cloths for communion, washed and pressed the garments for baptisms, and wrote down, in tidy script, who would sit with the widow this week and who would take the children on Saturday so she could sleep. Their leadership ran the rails of care and order: who needs soup; who needs a visit; who needs a stern word softened by tea; who needs the deacon; who needs the pastor; who needs a ride to the doctor; who needs a place to stay. Ask anyone and they would say the pastor preached. Ask those who knew and they would add, "The mothers kept the church from falling apart."

When candidates came forward, the mothers' board received them first. Formation did not begin at the water; it began at the table. The questions were plain as weather and just as searching. "Do you know the Lord?"—not as a puzzle but as a Person met in trouble. "Do you forgive?"—the kind that requires a story before a yes can be trusted. "Can you be corrected?"—because a church without correction turns sour. "Will you come when we call?"—because belonging is not a mood. If a candidate needed time, they gave time, and gave a sponsor, and put the name on the early-morning list. When the day came, they stood at the water's edge, steadying hands on backs and shoulders, ready with towels, ready with blankets, ready with the right song as soon as the coughing stopped and the laughter started.

On communion weeks, they prepared the long table with more theology than talk. Bread without hurry. Cups counted twice. Basins and towels ready for feet if the service called for it. They had learned that holiness shows up in details: clean linens, quiet doors, a pitcher filled before it's needed, a hand on an elbow at the right moment. They watched the room while the deacons watched the plates and the pastor watched the text. If a child squirmed, a peppermint appeared. If a man trembled, a shawl slipped around his shoulders. If a woman wept, a handkerchief and a firm hand arrived together. They did not need the title "theologian." They had the work.

By week's end, the catechism taught at the table had been tested in the band and practiced at the font and the rail. What began as "I believe" grew ribs: "We ask," "We wait," "We share," "We forgive," "We endure." It also grew legs: visits made, meals carried, sheets changed, floors swept, school fees pooled, funerals organized with dignity for those who could not afford it, a new mother's laundry done before she had to ask. If anyone wanted to know the church's doctrine, the women could hand them a page. If anyone wanted to see it, they could hand them a list of names and the week's assignments.

So much of the church's stability lived where few histories look—at stoves, in back rooms, on porches, on the first pew to the left where the mothers sat, two seats in and two seats out, always leaving space for the one who would need to slip in late. They taught a creed that could be recited under breath while peeling potatoes, rocking a baby, waiting in a hallway outside a courtroom. They showed that prayer is not only what you say to God; it is what you do next for God's people. And when the young stood at the water or knelt at the rail, they stood and knelt inside a net the women had tied long before: strong, flexible, and ready to hold.

A people's Bible in song and story

Where paper was scarce or clipped, Scripture found a wider field: sung in lines the body could carry, stepped in circles that taught patience and courage, testified in sentences no one could refute. Exodus became a verb, Daniel a guarantee, Acts a map. Doctrine lived in the reply—"yes," "amen," "again"—and what the room would not answer did not become law.

The voice that learned to answer in yards and night meetings now raises beams and hangs doors. From yard school to sanctuary, from circle to city block, the people build houses strong enough to hold what they have already believed out loud. Next, the faith they voiced becomes wood and glass and weekly order: ushers and choirs, covenants and minutes, basements and bells—the architecture of a people who know how to stand together.

From control to conscience

What arrived as a tool of control—short questions, shorter answers, curated pages—left the yard in a different shape: the people's conscience. In circles and kitchens, the catechism moved from memory drill to moral backbone, tested by testimony, adjusted by proverb, and sealed in shared promise. The same form that once pressed toward quiet grew a spine; it learned to say deliver, endure, forgive, rise.

Chapter 8

Faith Transformed

The wood of the meetinghouse groaned when winter winds pressed against its clapboards. Inside, a white pastor read from a leather-bound Bible in a voice trained to be firm but not loud. On one side of the aisle sat white families on polished benches. In the gallery, up a narrow stair, Black men and women listened with bodies that knew the difference between endurance and submission. When the minister chose "Servants, obey," the words fell like sleet. When the psalm said, "He brought them out with a mighty hand," heads lifted as if the forecast had suddenly changed. The same Book spoke in two directions at once. On Monday, both readings would be remembered—but not equally. The gallery would keep the line about the hand that brings out.

This is the story of how Christianity in the American colonies and early United States became both a chain and a key, and how a people learned to tell which was which.

Fire in the Text: Exodus as Map, Moses as Method

By the mid-eighteenth century, itinerant revivalists crisscrossed the colonies—field preachers with lung power and urgency. Their sermons flattened classes and awakened conscience. For many enslaved hearers, this wave of preaching did two things at once. It announced a God who knew names and counted tears. It brought into sharper relief the unholy arguments that said bondage was good for the soul.[44]

In cabins and quarters, biblical interpretation found muscle. Exodus ceased to be ancient history and became a working map. "Let my people go" was tested as a prayer in the field, a whisper in a kitchen, and a line lifted in a watch-night service. It held in all three places. Deliverance became a verb, not a lecture. The story tightened its grip on practice: Passover nights of low talk and packed bundles; rehearsed routes under stars; quiet agreements made under the noise of a white preacher's benediction.

Other texts joined Exodus at the center of gravity. Joseph taught skill and restraint—how to live in a house that wasn't yours, keep your body, and save what you could. Daniel carried courage in the face of teeth and fire. Acts sketched the fellowship of those who owned nothing and shared everything. Psalms gave complaint permission and praise a drumbeat even when drums were banned. A distinctive reading took form: God is not the sponsor of the strong; God is the ally of the bound. Holiness looks like truth-telling, mutual aid, and an open path out of Egypt when it comes.

Two Pulpits in One Room

As Black attendance grew in white congregations, "accommodation" took formal shape. Galleries were added for Black worshipers; separate class meetings were assigned; Black exhorters were allowed to encourage but seldom to teach audibly to whites. During communion, seating arrangements were as legible as the creed. Some pastors believed they were offering equal grace in unequal times. Black members felt the doctrine of the day in the muscles of the back and the ache of the neck. Partition teaches its own theology.[45]

Still, a second pulpit stood within the first: testimony. When time was given for "remarks," the grammar of the service changed. A woman stood and said, "He kept me." A man said, "I forgave," and the room learned what the sermon meant by mercy. A youth recited a verse and then told how he refused to steal when ordered to bring home another man's crop. The congregation witnessed exegesis by life—Scripture read aloud in the accents of experience. When the benediction came, white hearers filed out talking about application points. Black hearers climbed down the narrow stair carrying sentences with edges on them.[46]

Religion as Harness—and Knife

Planters learned early how piety could quiet hands. Approved homilies, plantation "sabbaths," and carefully supervised baptisms functioned as reins. Duty texts were chosen; dangerous texts were left for heaven. Some colonists wrote plainly that religion kept "the more unruly in good order." Others described the enslaved as "children," requiring "simple instruction" but not the "temptations" of Exodus or Acts. For every ledger that recorded cloth and corn, another script recorded verses to be read—tools intended to bind as surely as rope.

The rope frayed under scrutiny. Enslaved readers—many illiterate in letters, but not in sense—held texts up to deeds. When a master punished for a prayer, the sermon about kindness lost its grammar. When a revivalist wept at the altar and did not flinch at the block, the tears were weighed and found thin. Whenever a text that demanded obedience was read, a choir of counter-texts joined it in memory: "You shall not steal," "Do not oppress the stranger," "Proclaim liberty throughout the land." Religion as harness could be cut by religion as knife, if the hand holding it was sure.

"It Was the Spirit Made Me See": Rebellion and Revelation

Not all resistance spoke in doctrine. Some spoke in visions. Two names—and two moments—embodied a frightening clarity to the white imagination and a severe hope to many Black believers: Denmark Vesey

(1822) and Nat Turner (1831). Both men read the Bible as a book with orders. Vesey, a free Black carpenter and churchman in Charleston, read Exodus with razor precision. He saw Israel's route in street maps and believed deliverance hinged not on permission but on daring. He cited Scripture to justify plans to strike and flee. His letters and meetings alarmed informers; the plot was uncovered; the trials wrapped Scripture in iron as evidence of guilt. White readers scrawled warnings on the Book: do not let them read this way. Black readers held it closer.[47]

Turner, enslaved in Southampton County, dreamed and saw signs. The sun darkened; letters were written in blood upon leaves; voices pressed him to act. He preached, baptized, and in late August led an uprising that left dozens dead and the countryside in fear. Court records name his visions and his citations—Luke's "greater than these," Revelation's white horse, the God who "has made bare His holy arm." White chroniclers called him fanatic. Black hearers understood the grammar even if they would not choose the form. The Spirit that quickened a body under song could also quicken to the sword. Many recoiled at the cost. Few believed the readings were baseless.[48]

The response was swift and severe: new laws against assembly and literacy; tighter patrols; suspicious eyes on every prayer meeting; sermons issued from courthouse pulpits arguing that God's Israel lived north of the Mason-Dixon line, not in the quarters. At the same time, free Black communities and some white allies doubled down on catechism and preaching—the kind that taught hearts to be brave without breaking, and tongues to say liberty without indiscretion. The Bible did not change. Access to it did.

Households of Their Own: From Galleries to Sanctuaries

By the 1780s and 1790s, Black Methodists and Baptists from Philadelphia to Savannah had begun to form class meetings, mutual aid societies, and then churches under Black leadership. Gallery religion did not suffice for people who had learned to preach with their bodies. Walkouts—peaceful but firm—shaped new institutions. Mother Bethel in Philadelphia (African Methodist Episcopal) and African Baptist churches in the South wrote covenants in plain hands: discipline, care, freedom to choose when to speak and how loud.

The theology in those rooms bore a distinct accent. God is holy, yes, and that holiness is not antiseptic. It is partial to the bruised. Sin is both personal wrongdoing and a structure that trains the strong to forget the weak. Salvation is reconciliation to God and to neighbors in shared bread, pooled coins, and a steady campaign against chains. Holiness is not only sobriety; it is courage. The Spirit does not only comfort; the Spirit empowers. The church is not only a soul's hospital; it is a school for freedom—with rules, minutes, and a benevolence fund.

Membership records in these congregations read like weather logs: "Sister —— received on profession of faith, gives out hymns on first Sundays;" "Brother —— restored after confession; promises restitution;" "Collected for widow ——: $3.12." Tucked between names lie the real creeds: "The poor have the gospel preached," "All have gifts," "We will walk together." White missionaries' reports, read alongside these minutes, tell two stories: surprise at the fervor, and dismay at autonomy. The same fervor that warmed revival tents made white trustees uneasy when directed toward independent governance.

The High Cost of Reading—and the Higher Cost of Silence

In the wake of Vesey and Turner, literacy bans spread. Some argued that hearing was enough for faith; others demanded that only authorized readings be allowed. Black teachers answered with patience and audacity. Lessons were tucked into chores: letters scratched in ash, syllables counted in corn, numbers learned in pew counts and offering plates. Slave narratives later recalled these hours as both terror and light—masters' rages, secret alphabets, first sentences read by candle stubs. Many testified that Scripture read in one's own mouth changes the spine. You cannot un-know that "all" means "all" once you hear yourself say it.

Counter-readings matured. A planter's diary might record "seditious singing—Moses, Daniel," as if names themselves were contraband. A missionary might write, "The people delight in the darker prophets," meaning those who threaten kings. In testimony and narratives, the enslaved described night meetings not as frenzy, but as clarity: God's justice is the measure of man's laws; suffering is neither romantic nor permanent; persons are not property because God will not be the owner of owners.

The Sermon of the Everyday: Work, Rest, and Sanctioned Subversion

Between courts and covenants, a daily theology worked like yeast. Low-talk alliances defended Sunday as more than a rest—sacred time, not "idle." Naming the day set a limit to the master's reach, one that God Himself set. Prayer before meals—sometimes silent, sometimes a word—declared that food is not wages only; it is gift. Borrowing and lending operated by a code closer to Acts than to debtor's prison. Weddings—whether recognized by law or not—became covenantal, vowed before God and a crowd who would enforce the promise when law would not. Funerals, often at night, transformed sorrow into conspiracy against despair. Every rite of passage preached. "We will not be small," they said, "even here."

The Grammar of Resistance: Quiet, Loud, and Everything Between

Religion's role in resistance ranged from quiet sabotage to bolt-upright revolt. A hymn slowed a task. A prayer prolonged a meeting. A fast shamed a steward. A reading from Exodus hardened a plan. When rebellion broke, religion provided signals, schedules, and sanction. When revolt failed, religion stitched the survivors back together and forbade cynicism from becoming creed. To choose Exodus as the master text was to choose a posture: God can and will act; we must stay ready to walk.

Even in quieter seasons, Black churches functioned as training grounds in self-government. Elections were held; disagreements were aired then bounded; funds were accounted for; offenders admonished then restored. This discipline made public action possible later. It also gave ordinary saints the sense that they were citizens in the kingdom now, not merely in heaven later. The gallery had been antechamber. The sanctuary was a house. A people stood taller when they carried their own keys.

The White Gaze—and the Mirror

White accounts of slave religion often reflect more about the writer than the worshiper. Some saw "enthusiasm," which meant too much emotion for good sense. Others saw hypocrisy when a doctor's bill was paid by the same man who held a woman's life in lien. There were exceptions—pastors and missionaries who told the truth both directions and risked for it. But most records require double reading: note what they fear, note what they admire, and then read between their lines for what the people were doing while they were writing. The mirror is cloudy, but it shows enough.

Slave narratives shine clearer. In them, prayers are not props; they are breath. Sermons are not entertainment; they are lanterns. Songs are not noise; they are archives. Court records from rebellion trials are cold, but they name the words the men spoke and the texts they believed. Put these alongside early membership rolls, minutes, and covenant statements, and a textured picture emerges: a Christianity tested like iron on anvil, shaped by blows, and turned toward freedom even when shackled.

The Turn toward Houses—the Turn toward History

By 1860, the landscape had shifted. Independent Black congregations in the North purchased buildings, printed minutes, sent delegates to conventions, and founded schools. In the South, under law and patrol, the work went on with less paper and more memory, but the shape was the same: a people knitting a church that could carry both Sunday and Monday, both Exodus and Matthew 5, both the promise of later and the demand of now.

Faith had been forced into a corner. It learned to fight there—without losing mercy. It learned to read there—without losing wonder. It learned to build there—without permission. The transformation was not from "African to Christian" or from "heathen to civilized," as the pamphlets bragged. It was from gallery to sanctuary, from being read to to reading aloud, from a catechism strapped to a master's will to a creed bound to a living God.

Bridge: From Voice to Architecture

The next step belongs to wood and stone. The people who learned to answer "amen" together will raise beams together. Brush arbors become framed houses; framed houses become brick sanctuaries with bells to call the city. The aisles are laid for processions; the pools for baptism; the lofts for choirs; the basements for kitchens and schools. Mothers' boards and deacons' benches stand where the gallery once stood. The faith forged in the open finds rooms strong enough to hold it. From voice to architecture, the doctrine of deliverance takes up a city block—and invites the neighborhood in.

Part III

Freedom and Institution Building

Books By Rene'

Chapter 9

Breaking Away

The morning the ushers tried to pull the kneeling men up by their coats, a line broke that would not be mended. St. George's Methodist Episcopal Church in Philadelphia had a gallery for Black worshipers and rules for where to sit and when to pray. On that Sunday, Richard Allen and Absalom Jones knelt anyway—where there was room, where God was—and white stewards hustled over to correct them. "You must not kneel here." The men finished their prayers, stood, and walked out with the Black members behind them. On the street, they did not yet have a pulpit, a building, or a name. They had the one thing without which none of the rest matters: agreement.[49]

The Free African Society: From Mutual Aid to Ecclesial Choice

In 1787 Allen and Jones helped found the Free African Society, a non-denominational aid circle dedicated to relief, education, and dignity. They organized visits to the sick, pooled money for funerals, supported fugitives arriving from the South, and trained children to read. When yellow fever raged in 1793, they remained in the city, nursing neighbors and burying the dead while others fled. They also argued—sometimes gently, sometimes like men with a time limit—about what sort of church their people should build. Jones leaned Anglican; Allen, Methodist. Both agreed on this much: the new house must be free of white control. The society was the halfway land where a people learned to govern themselves before they took on the weight of weekly worship.

Absalom Jones and St. Thomas: Black Episcopalians Claim the Rail

By 1792, Jones led the formation of the African Episcopal Church of St. Thomas, the first Black Episcopal congregation in the United States. Two years later he was ordained deacon and, in 1802, priest—the first African American to wear that collar. St. Thomas embraced order and sacrament with a seriousness born of exclusion. Its members built a sanctuary, wrote a constitution, and stood at a rail that had once been closed to them. They used the theological ideal of "catholicity"—a church for all—to demand recognition from a denomination that prized bishops and canons. They received that recognition in part because they could not be ignored any longer. Their altar taught a city that dignity and discipline belonged wherever faith gathered in truth.[50]

Mother Bethel and the AME: Allen's Long Lawsuit and a New Connection

Allen remained Methodist by conviction and temperament—plain preaching, vigorous singing, a gospel aimed at the conscience and the street. He bought a lot on Sixth and Lombard and, with help from friends and stubborn labor, raised a wooden church in 1794: Bethel. White Methodists tried to keep the new congregation under their trustees' thumb—appointing Allen's preachers, interfering in finances, and ultimately putting Bethel up for auction. Allen sued, won, lost, and sued again. In 1815 he bought back his own church; in 1816, the Pennsylvania Supreme Court finally affirmed Bethel's right to govern itself. That same month he convened ministers from Black Methodist churches in Philadelphia, Baltimore, Wilmington, Salem, and Attleborough. Together they organized the African Methodist Episcopal Church, the first fully independent Black denomination in the United States, and elected Allen bishop. The connection spread quickly: first across the mid-Atlantic, then into the Ohio country, and, against all odds, into slave states where law and patrols watched every meeting.[51]

"We Will Serve the Lord": Black Baptists and Congregational Freedom

Alongside Methodist and Episcopal formations, independent Black Baptist churches grew from class meetings and brush arbors into covenanted congregations. In Petersburg, Virginia, First Baptist (organized by 1774) and Gillfield Baptist (1797) moved into town in the early republic and built their own houses. In northern cities, free Black Baptists wrote church covenants with the clearest ink in America: we will walk together; we will discipline in love; we will care for the poor; we will keep each other to our vows. Minutes show the muscle and mercy of the congregational way—debts settled, quarrels reconciled, gifts recognized, women licensed to exhort, and men restored after repentance. Where bishops and conferences were not available or not trusted, the vote and the covenant did the work of order.[52]

Organization: The Blessings and Burdens of Independence

Autonomy solved indignity; it did not solve poverty. Buildings needed beams and bricks; pastors needed support; widows needed coal; schools needed slates. Within a decade, most independent churches had deacons' funds, mothers' boards, and committees to mind the poor. They drew up constitutions, printed minutes, and stitched hymnals that bound spirituals to Watts and Wesley. They also faced external pressures: white trustees who wanted to "help" by holding keys, denominational officials who feared losing Black members, and newspapers that called any Black assembly suspect. Leadership faltered at times. Pastors burned out. Factions formed. The miracle is not that they argued; it is that they kept minutes and reconciled.

The Church as City: Schools, Aid, and the Underground Line

By the 1810s–1820s, church basements in Philadelphia, New York, Boston, Providence, and Pittsburgh functioned like civic switchboards: Sabbath schools taught basic literacy from spellers and primers; weekday lectures featured physicians on smallpox, lawyers on manumission papers, and abolitionists on petition strategy; benevolent societies distributed flour, coal, and work lists timed to harsh winters. Sanctuaries doubled as mutual-aid treasuries and, when required, as safe rooms on the Underground Railroad—trapdoors, back rooms, and cemetery sheds repurposed to hold fugitives between dusk and the first bell. The rails between altar and street ran both ways: hymns and minutes at one end, vigilance committees and lodging tickets at the other.

Newspapers and Letters: Announcing Separation, Explaining Hope

Pamphlets and newspapers chronicled these separations with equal parts alarm and respect. White editors alternated between fretting over "schism" and praising "orderly conduct;" Black editors printed constitutions, notices of meetings, ordination reports, and lists of benevolence receipts and disbursements. Richard Allen's Life, Experience, and Gospel Labours framed withdrawal as obedience to conscience and a simple demand for un-humiliated worship. Across private letters, the texture appears in small requests and corrections: loans to finish roofs, appeals for teachers, warnings to cool a zealous deacon, thanks for a week's wood and a winter's coal. The paper trail reads like institutional catechism: Why separate? To worship without insult; to govern with integrity; to care for the poor with the people's own hands.

Theology in the Ledger: What the Records Reveal

Early minute books preach a plain theology of covenant and discipline. Entries receive members on profession of faith, exclude and later restore the intemperate, collect for widows and apprenticeships, and assign days of prayer for the enslaved. Votes authorize petitions to legislatures for schools, allocate deacons' funds, and commission itinerants to new towns. Methodist class tickets, Baptist covenants, and Episcopal vestry minutes converge on the same doctrinal practice: holiness enforced by habit, mercy paired with accountability, mission funded by coins counted at wooden tables. Borrowing ran both directions—Methodists learning congregational accountability, Baptists adapting class-meeting intimacy, Episcopalians leaning on mutual-aid rigor—while mothers' boards quietly set the weekly cadence of visitation, relief, and instruction.

Frontier and Tidewater: Stretching the Map

As canals and roads opened west, itinerant preachers carried minutes, hymn tunes, and constitutions into Ohio, Indiana, and the Old Northwest, organizing in schoolhouses and borrowed halls until a frame building could be raised. In Maryland, Delaware, Kentucky, and the Tidewater, Black Methodists and Baptists gathered under license where possible and beyond it when necessary, balancing visibility with safety. Reports from these circuits are flinty and pastoral: "Send tracts and coats;" "Two baptized through the ice;" "The sheriff attends and has not yet troubled us." To the north, communities in Canada West formed new conferences for those who chose safety across the border over life under kidnapping threats and Black laws. Congregations mapped themselves along waterways and turnpikes like a chain of beacons: prayer, vote, collection, construction.

Black Baptists: Congregational Freedom, Local Muscle

Independent Black Baptist churches matured alongside the Methodist and Episcopal streams. In Petersburg, First Baptist (organized by 1774) and Gillfield (1797) moved from brush arbors into town, building houses and drafting covenants that pledged mutual care, disciplined charity, and public order. In northern cities, congregational minutes display muscle and mercy: debts settled by subscription; quarrels reconciled after council; women licensed to exhort; repentant men restored after public confession. Where episcopal or conference structures were absent or suspect, the vote, the covenant, and the church meeting shouldered governance. Association meetings stitched congregations together, exchanging letters of fellowship, pulpit supply, and relief for distressed members.

Organization: Blessings and Burdens of Independence

Autonomy cured humiliation but not scarcity. Beams, bricks, coal, slates, and salaries demanded steady collections. Within a few years, most churches carried deacons' funds, mothers' boards, building committees, and poor committees; they printed constitutions and annual minutes; they stitched hymnals that set Watts and Wesley alongside spiritual refrains. External pressures persisted: white "trustees" offering help in exchange for keys, denominational officials anxious about losing Black members, and municipal authorities inclined to treat any Black assembly as suspect. Internal strains surfaced—pastor fatigue, factionalism, class tensions, and color hierarchies—but the notable fact is procedural fidelity: arguments ended with motions, votes, and reconciliations entered in ink.

Women's Work: The Quiet Engine

Across denominations, women's labor made independence durable. Sewing circles turned fabric into operating budgets; visiting societies mapped needs block by block; sabbath-school teachers multiplied literacy; mothers' boards enforced quiet standards of care and correction. Fund-raising suppers financed stoves, pew repairs, and the first books for congregational libraries. Widows' mites, repeated across a hundred kitchens, retired mortgages and underwrote itinerant travel. The record lines may be short—"Paid Sister —— $2 for wood"—but the accumulated effect is architectural.

Discipline, Dignity, and Public Reputation

Discipline remained both moral and strategic. Temperance protected limited wages; marriage discipline rebuilt family stability after sale and separation; savings and punctuality answered slander with evidence. Public order mattered: starting meetings on time, keeping peace without constables, paying debts, and publishing financial statements built reputations that won grudging civic respect and, at times, essential toleration. During epidemics and riots, churches organized nurses, burial teams, and watch committees, embodying public virtue before the city reciprocated with public rights.

Allen's Lawsuits and a New Connection

The Bethel property struggle—white trustees attempting to control appointments and finances, even pushing for auction—pressed Allen into court, where defeat, purchase, appeal, and eventual vindication taught congregations to hold deeds, draft charters carefully, and litigate when required. The 1816 gathering of ministers from Philadelphia, Baltimore, Wilmington, Salem, and Attleborough did not invent independence; it standardized it. The new African Methodist Episcopal Church supplied bishops from the people's own ranks, itinerancy by Black appointment, publishing programs, and discipline adapted to the needs at hand. It spread mid-Atlantic first, then along river towns into the Ohio country, and—where law allowed or could be skirted—into slave states under wary patrols.

Why It Mattered: Autonomy as Discipleship

"Breaking away" was a theological choice expressed in institutional form. A people who could choose leaders, discipline members, care for the poor from their own treasury, and send preachers where conscience pointed enacted a New Testament pattern and countered a civic order that consigned them to balconies and edges. Every deed recorded in Black hands redrew the civic map; every clerk's entry recording a vote chaired by a Black moderator documented resistance; every pulpit that preached deliverance in a Black voice insisted that gospel authority and Black dignity were not at odds. The houses stood; the covenants bound; the benches filled. The next pressure point would be public life—schools and conventions, temperance and colonization debates, antislavery petitions and revivals—where these churches would remain sanctuaries and become headquarters.

The infrastructure is in place: hymnals, minutes, benevolence ledgers, property deeds, itinerant routes, and a community trained to deliberate. The question ahead is how far these tools can move a nation—how pulpits, prayer meetings, church basements, and association hallways become stations, committees, conventions, and platforms for an organized moral assault on slavery and its laws.

Chapter 10

Preaching Freedom

Stations and Signals: Churches as Underground Hubs

By the 1830s, basements that once held coal and hymnals also held maps, passwords, and bundles of clothing labeled for "friends from Maryland," turning sanctuaries into stations on an improvised interstate of mercy. Vigilance committees posted watch near ferry slips and depots; sextons learned to lift floorboards as deftly as they set communion rails. Weeknight prayer schedules became cover for arrivals after last light, with matrons assigning beds and ushers repurposing collection baskets as ration kits. Pastors taught discretion as a discipline: speak little, write less, remember everything necessary and nothing that could hang a neighbor.[53]

Pulpit to Platform: Ministers as Abolitionists

A generation of Black ministers carried sermons beyond their pulpits to lyceums, antislavery halls, and convention floors where biblical text met statute law in a contest for allegiance. Henry Highland Garnet, Samuel Ringgold Ward, and their peers pitted Exodus and the prophets against slave codes, insisting that the God who judged Pharaoh would not bless a republic of auction blocks. The cadences honed in Sabbath services—call and response, plain application, a conscience pressed to decision—proved equally suited to a lecture circuit linked by steamboats and editorial offices. The pulpit produced platforms; the amen converted to a signature on petitions.

Bible and Bondage: Theological Arguments for Freedom

Preaching freedom required more than outrage; it required exegesis that could withstand debate in parlors and courts. Sermons dismantled "curse of Ham" folklore with careful readings; they set Paul's household codes in their historical frame and pulled Philemon forward as a plea for manumission grounded in brotherhood. Exodus functioned as a master key, paired with Christ's inaugural in Luke—"liberty to the captives"—to define slavery as sin and emancipation as repentance. In church classrooms, youth learned to argue chapter and verse, not as abstraction but as instruction for jury boxes and town meetings where scripture still set terms for public morality.[54]

Networks: Denominations, Press, and Passage

Denominational connections—AME itinerancy, Baptist associations, Episcopal rector networks—became arteries for news, personnel, and money. A visiting elder could carry a name safely between cities; a quarterly meeting could double as an intelligence exchange; a printed discipline could tuck a letter inside its pasteboard. Newspapers aligned with churches multiplied that reach, blending sermons, meeting notices, escape narratives, and legal alerts into a weekly rhythm of mobilization. The same routes that moved hymnals moved people, and the same presses that set verses set broadsides warning of kidnappers and new state laws.[55]

Risk and Response: Law, Patrols, and Church Defense

With risk elevated, congregations adapted. Door wardens learned to ask the right questions; night watch committees shared whistles and lantern codes; treasurers kept a small purse uncounted on public ledgers for emergencies. When authorities raided on rumor, choir lofts hid documents and matrons diverted attention with rehearsals that ran long and loud. Pastors mastered the art of the affidavit, swearing to baptisms and marriages to shore up claims of free status; deacons learned court corridors, bail terms, and the cost in coin and reputation of a mistrusted name. Worship and wariness lived in the same hallway.

Women at the Core: Hospitality, Intelligence, and Fundraising

Women's boards stabilized operations that courage needed to survive more than a week. They ran clothing drives sized for travel, stocked infirmary baskets with salves and broth, and turned sewing circles into information exchanges that mapped alleys as accurately as any survey. Their fairs raised funds without calling attention; their visits verified whether a new face belonged to a cousin or a catcher's decoy. When meetings closed, many walked home with a girl or boy at the elbow, teaching along the way how to look behind, how to step through a shadow, and how to sing softly enough not to carry past the next corner.[56]

Schoolrooms, Lecterns, and Law

Education remained the lever that could move both souls and statutes. Sabbath schools expanded into evening grammar and arithmetic classes; lecture series brought physicians, printers, and attorneys into sanctuaries to teach hygiene, typesetting, and petition drafting. Churches organized reading circles around antislavery pamphlets and legal manuals, making law less a threat and more a tool. Youth drilled elocution on abolition poetry and psalms alternately, learning that a good sentence could open a heart or close a cross-examination.

Prayer Meetings and Petitions

The same hands that rose in prayer also signed petitions to statehouses and Congress, connecting devotion to procedure. Fast days declared in congregational meetings prepared hearts and headlines for the delivery of signatures bound in twine; testimonies given at the rail reappeared condensed into memorials that pleaded for jury trials for alleged fugitives, repeal of Black laws, and the protection of free papers. The ledger of intercession and the ledger of signatures often matched columns: a widow prayed for her son's safety on Tuesday and signed for his legal shelter on Thursday.

Preaching Style and Public Imagination

The sound of the movement shaped its reach. Revival cadences carried into street rallies; the sermon's turn from doctrine to exhortation translated into the oration's pivot from evidence to appeal. Imagery drawn from Jordan crossings and fiery furnaces made legal abstractions visible to listeners who had seen rivers and fires of their own. Hymns did political work: verses adapted on the fly turned meetings into rehearsals for courage, locking memory to melody for the hard walk home past hostile corners.

Dissent, Strategy, and the Pulpit

Strategy disputes visited the churches that housed the cause. Some pastors urged moral suasion and refused any hint of violence; others, following Garnet's sharper line, allowed that self-defense and flight required more than patient appeals. Pulpits hosted debates that would have torn less practiced communities; minutes recorded motions to support lecturers, with provisos about tone and venue. Even when tempers rose, procedure held—motions, seconds, votes—and then the closing hymn, not as avoidance but as a way to set contention inside a larger obedience.

Southward Currents: Preaching Under Watch

In border and slave states, churches improvised under surveillance. Licensed Black preachers learned to read a room under a sheriff's gaze; prayer lines doubled as messengers' queues; baptisms in creeks provided opportunities for whispered directions between verses. White allies varied—some lent barns and legal names, others locked doors at the first rumor—but even unreliable help could be staged around with timing and a spare key. Travel journals from itinerants read like coded devotionals: "The brethren stand," "We sang low," "Two were added."

Money, Deeds, and Motion

The movement cost money as predictably as a roof in winter. Collections earmarked "mission" shifted by month between hymnals, legal fees, travel fare, and sacks of flour for a family that had lost a wage earner to jail. Trustees learned to insulate properties from seizure; lawyers in pews advised on incorporations built to withstand hostile courts. A treasurer's steady hand could be the difference between a case lost for lack of bond and a dawn train caught with a valid ticket.

Print, Reputation, and Protection

Public reputation protected as surely as lock and key. Churches published audited accounts, attendance norms, and relief lists to display order to neighbors inclined to suspect conspiracies. Respectability could not stop a mob, but it persuaded judges and aldermen who preferred quiet streets that these congregations were guardians of the peace, not hosts to crime. When riots came, pastors lifted walking-sticks in defense and lifted voices after for restraint and rebuilding, writing letters that named injuries without surrendering to vengeance.

Sabbath to Weekday: Seamless Work

By the early 1860s, the week's calendar showed no clean line between liturgy and logistics. Sunday's sermon offered a text for Monday's committee; Tuesday's prayer fueled Wednesday's petition; Thursday's choir practice masked a meeting; Friday's fast steadied Saturday's rescue planning. The doors went out and in as often for meetings as for worship, a rhythm that tired feet but trained a people to take instruction, keep confidence, and act together under pressure.

On the Eve of War

When national crisis opened into war, these churches already knew how to drill hearts and hands. They had officers accustomed to minutes and to midnight; they had treasurers used to stretching coins and to raising sudden subscriptions; they had singers who could hold a note while trouble passed the door. The networks, habits, and courage formed under the burden of patrols and laws were ready to become hospitals, recruitment halls, and relief depots—institutions that would meet a new set of needs without abandoning the old call: to preach freedom and practice it, line by line and life by life.

Chapter 11

Reconstruction Faith

The great building

In the months after Appomattox, congregations organized faster than carpenters could keep pace, trading brush arbors for frames and, as soon as credit and collections allowed, for brick and lime. The new sanctuaries functioned as more than worship halls: they were addresses in law, centers of gravity in neighborhoods, and proofs that freedom had a street corner and a deed. Membership rolls swelled as spouses reunited and children raised on different plantations found their families' names written together at last; class systems and conference routines scaled up to keep order around baptisms, funerals, marriages, and constant relief. A bell that once summoned labor now set a community's schedule.

Schools below the sanctuary

Education ran through these churches like a load-bearing beam. Before paint dried upstairs, basements filled with benches, slates, and spellers. Teachers came from everywhere the moment would allow: northern missionary societies and denominational boards; army chaplains on extended furloughs; free Black instructors from cities; pastors, deacons, and their spouses who learned pedagogy one lesson ahead. Sabbath schools taught catechism and letters; evening classes met after fieldwork; summer "normal" institutes trained local teachers so schools did not fail when northern support shifted. Reading turned from ornament to infrastructure—necessary for petitions, contracts, and the ballot, and for a theology that insisted God addressed a people able to answer in writing.

From pulpit to polls

Sanctuary platforms became rostrums for political education. Mass meetings explained voter registration, constitutional conventions, and the responsibilities of office; pastors moderated with the same procedural steadiness used in conference; ushers managed entrances and lines; choirs steadied crowds asked to endure long agendas. Deacons chaired ward committees; trustees learned county ledgers; sextons, who once worked in shadows, kept keys and schedules for gatherings that would have been illegal only months before. The ritual of "motion, second, vote" traveled seamlessly between congregational business and courthouse forums, training civic habit in a people whose political lives had been deliberately starved.

Denominations on the move

Existing Black denominations—African Methodist Episcopal, African Methodist Episcopal Zion, independent and associational Baptists—extended rapidly into the South. Bishops assigned presiding elders to circuits that braided towns and countryside; missionary boards printed tracts and disciplines in cheap editions that could survive hard travel; hymnals rode in carpetbags beside legal forms. Associations of Black Baptists multiplied as congregations shucked white supervision and covenanted to govern themselves by vote, discipline, and mutual aid. Polity that protected dignity in Northern cities translated into rural routines sturdy enough for counties rebuilding from war: itinerancy paired with local trustees strong enough to hold property, hire and dismiss pastors, and manage debt across crop cycles.[57]

Women's boards, constant work

Women's societies stabilized plans that courage alone could not keep solvent. Sewing circles turned cloth into shingles and stoves, then into teachers' stipends; visiting bands surveyed need block by block and lane by lane; mothers' boards enforced quiet standards of decorum that built a public reputation for sobriety and care. Fund-raising fairs and church teas financed desks, fences, and first libraries: shelves of spellers, arithmetic manuals, geographies, and bound sermons. In many places, the women's meeting became the weekly anchor; the men's committee rotated, but the women's board did not adjourn.[58]

Freedmen's Bureau and the ledger

Where possible, pastors and trustees partnered with federal agents to secure school buildings, salaries, rations, and protection. Arrangements were pragmatic: the congregation provided rooms, guardianship of property, and nightly security; the Bureau supplied pay, some books, and the authority to mediate with local officials. Ledgers from these partnerships carry the same signatures repeated line after line: a practical record of a federal-ecclesial collaboration that extended beyond ideology into daily logistics. When federal support receded, treasurers shifted columns, reduced hours rather than closing schools, and solicited aid from denominational boards and city allies.[59]

Order, temperance, and respectability

Moral discipline took on public purpose. Temperance protected wages in a cash-poor economy where a day's drink could mean a week's lost rent; marriage discipline rebuilt family stability after separation and sale; punctuality and audited accounts answered slander with evidence. Printed minutes and subscription lists taught neighbors and officials that these congregations kept promises and paid debts. A reputation for order did not dissolve hostility, but it moved ambivalent magistrates and merchants toward toleration. Pastors linked sanctification to freedom's maintenance: holiness kept money in the house, children in school, and anglers for labor at bay.

Violence, vigilance, and faith

Opposition organized almost as quickly as revivals. Night riders tested doors; sheriffs tested permits; arson tested rafters and resolve. Churches adapted: watch committees rotated through the week; insurance policies spread risk; duplicate records went home with clerks each night. Leaders learned to file affidavits promptly, to testify without naming those who could not be protected, and to collect statements when local authorities refused to witness assaults. Prayers for enemies sat beside petitions for protection; forgiveness did not preclude legal complaint. Congregations sang benedictions in sanctuaries repaired from ash and returned to their calendars as proof that the lampstand had not been moved.

Union Leagues and church rhythms

Political clubs borrowed church cadence—scripture before resolutions, call-and-response to fix key points, hymns after speeches to hold a crowd through fatigue and fear. Pastors preached civic duty as stewardship of a blood-bought trust; deacons organized rides to courthouse steps; teachers tutored new voters on ballot forms and the fine print of labor contracts.

Ritual made the unfamiliar legible and managed; the sanctuary made the political safe enough to practice. When elections approached, midweek services functioned as rehearsals: how to face intimidation, how to answer a challenge, how to stand in line without taking a taunt to heart.[60]

Property, debt, and durability

Ownership remained the hinge on which independence swung. Trustees learned title, lien, release, and foreclosure, adding a vocabulary of risk to the old grammar of covenant. Mortgages were retired with bazaars and building funds; pew rentals gave way to free sittings as voluntary giving stabilized. Some debts outpaced optimism and required reorganization; others became the proof of a people's capacity to plan, sacrifice, and finish a communal project. A burned church rebuilt and a mortgage retired by nickels provided testimony stronger than most sermons: fidelity could turn coins into cornices.

Print and platform

Church newspapers and denominational minutes turned local labor into a southern conversation. Columns announced dedications, school exhibitions, revivals, and conference actions; obituaries honored teachers and deacons whose names might otherwise have gone no farther than the cemetery gate. Pamphlets addressed sharecropping contracts, temperance, marriage law, and voter intimidation; Sunday-school quarterlies synchronized lessons across miles and dialects. A press run of a thousand could change a county's plan; a hymn supplement could reset a region's sound; an annual minute proved growth to donors and courage to the newly organized.[61]

Migration and the map

Freedom redrew routes and expectations. Families moved from plantations to towns near depots; veterans followed comrades to levee work, turpentine camps, mills, and rail yards; teachers traced letters along lines of track. Churches followed and led: planting missions at junctions and river landings; raising frames as soon as a stove, a treasurer, and a class leader could be named. Northward migration laid new ties—letters, remittances, hymnals, exhorters—between southern sanctuaries and northern mother churches. The result was a lattice in which a member could travel three counties and recognize the order of service and the order of business.

Color lines inside and out

The public color line stood overt and brutal; inside churches, subtler lines of class, education, skin tone, and city-country habit required pastoral skill. Minutes show deliberate rotation of offices among trades and neighborhoods, explicit welcomes to migrants from different worship styles, and catechisms used to make doctrine common property regardless of schooling. Colorism received rebuke in sermons that insisted the font leveled distinctions; class pride met stories of the manger and fishermen-apostles. Unity did not erase difference, but it set common labor ahead of private precedence.

Children of the church

A generation grew up under bells, benches, and blackboards. Children memorized catechisms and readers, recited poems at school exhibitions in packed sanctuaries, and learned to sit through long meetings with their hands folded and their ears open. They learned to vote on motions in youth groups, to keep confidences that protected neighbors, and to sing harmony strong enough to carry a congregation through fire and harvest failure. By the 1890s, many of these children taught the next class, wrote the church's minutes, or took the pulpit from elders whose voices had carried through war and famine.

Rituals of restitution

Freedom required new rites of repair. "Reunion" services recognized marriages formed under slavery and rewove them under law; name-taking ceremonies gave children surnames chosen rather than assigned; memorial days recited the names of those lost by sale or war. Communion lines included veterans in faded coats and women who had kept households alive with gardens and washboards; baptisms in creeks drew crowds whose cheers sounded like homecoming. Ritual worked healing where law could not reach, and it taught a people how to remember without surrendering to bitterness.

Healing and health

Churches doubled as infirmaries in epidemics and steady clinics in between. Women's visiting societies kept baskets stocked with liniment, broth, and clean linen; pastors carried lists of the consumptive, the fevered, and the injured; lectures by physicians taught sanitation, vaccination, and basic first aid. Collections for medicine and burials appeared beside missions and schools, acknowledging that a sick body cannot read and a bereaved mother cannot attend night class. Cemeteries laid out with care embodied the conviction that the dead deserved order and honor no less than the living.

Labor and contracts

Sharecropping and wage labor required literate negotiation. Church meetings hosted contract readings; trustees reviewed clauses on liens, advances, and settlement; itinerant lecturers explained the meaning of "furnish" and the arithmetic of debt peonage. When disputes arose, deacons accompanied workers to magistrates; pastors wrote letters of character and attested to agreements. Sermons took up Proverbs on weights and measures, insisting that righteousness included full accounting in cotton and coin. Where possible, benevolent funds bridged gaps when employers delayed wages, preventing desperation sales or predatory loans.

Law and learning the state

Congregations learned the state as a terrain to be mapped. Clerks studied incorporation statutes and kept charters current; lay leaders learned jury duty and grand jury advocacy; pastors carried extracts of school and marriage laws folded into the back of their Bibles. Petitions for school funding and road maintenance bore church letterheads and dozens of signatures; complaints against sheriffs and constables followed formal channels. Even when rebuffed, the repetition taught people to inhabit citizenship as a muscle memory.

Music and memory

Reconstruction's soundscape mixed lined-out hymns, spirituals adapted for sanctuary use, and new compositions written for four-part choirs. Singing stitched together accents and geographies; it trained breath for long meetings and courage for short nights. Printed hymnals stabilized texts; memory kept melodies when torches found presses. Choirs functioned as training schools: punctuality, practice, intonation, and the fellowship that held a soprano and a bass in harmony despite arguments in the trustees' room.

Funerals, cemeteries, and continuity

Funerals carried theology into public view. Processions through town centered grief and insisted that lives lived in kitchens and fields deserved the dignity of measured pace and song. Cemeteries organized by churches created sacred geography: rows marked by hand-carved stones and scripture, plots purchased by those who had never before purchased anything that could not be taken. All Souls' observances rehearsed names so children would carry them forward; inscriptions taught literacy in stone: "Beloved teacher," "Deacon faithful," "Mother in Israel."

College from the classroom

Colleges often began in the corner of a sanctuary before moving to a frame, and then to a brick hall when subscriptions and denominational grants could be assembled. Catalogs listed preparatory, normal, and theological courses; libraries started with crates of cast-off volumes and grew into reading rooms with encyclopedias and atlases. Faculty wore many hats: preacher, principal, printer, fundraiser. Graduation exercises filled churches with families who had never seen a diploma; the benediction felt like a dedication for a future not previously imaginable.

Mission beyond the county

As institutions stabilized, congregations looked beyond county lines. Associations funded "home missions" to lumber camps, mining towns, and rail junctions; women's societies sent parcels to teachers in swamps and pine barrens; youth auxiliaries adopted projects—one schoolroom's desks, another's stove, a third's maps. Pastors exchanged pulpits across regions to spread ideas and renew courage. Lines of communication that carried prayer requests also carried supply lists, conference dates, and warnings about local hostility.

Facing retrenchment

As federal protection receded and "redeemers" regained office, churches absorbed new losses: teachers driven off, schoolhouses threatened, arrests on trivial pretexts, and tax schemes that shifted burdens onto Black property. The institutional response was steady rather than theatrical. Rebuild what burned; insure what stands; train more teachers locally; double mothers' aid; shorten night meetings when patrols grew bold; publish minutes anyway. Hope expressed itself in timetables, budget lines, and the stubborn insistence on ordinary faithfulness.

Print, reputation, and protection

Public reputation protected as surely as lock and key. Churches published audited accounts, attendance norms, and relief lists to demonstrate order to neighbors inclined to suspect conspiracies. Respectability could not stop a mob, but it persuaded judges and aldermen who preferred quiet that these congregations guarded the peace. After riots, letters named injuries without surrendering to vengeance, asking allies to stand forward and officials to enforce law. Editorials insisted that free worship and public education under church roofs were not threats but civic goods.

Rural circuits and endurance

Rural circuits demanded particular toughness. Preachers rode long loops, holding class meetings in kitchens and worship under pines; treasurers counted eggs and sweet potatoes beside coins; communion bread came from the nearest oven. Yet these small churches proved durable precisely because they were woven into daily work. When a storm knocked down rafters, the entire road crew belonged to the same class meeting; when a widow needed a roof, half the choir arrived with shingles. The circuit taught interdependence that would later sustain migration and urban ministry.

Urban congregations and complexity

In towns and cities, complexity pressed the calendar: day schools, night classes, benevolent boards, mutual aid lodges, youth societies, and temperance halls all competed for time and space. Pastors learned to be superintendents; trustees, property managers; deacons, caseworkers. Urban anonymity demanded new safeguards: membership interviews, letters of transfer, and clear lines between church charity and city poorhouses. The payoff was scale: a lecture could educate five hundred; a collection could fund a rural teacher for a term; a vigil could change a police chief's mind.

Ecumenical cooperation

Competition between denominations persisted, but cooperation grew where danger demanded it. Joint prayer meetings accompanied school dedications; pulpits exchanged lecturers for temperance, savings, and education campaigns; choirs joined for concerts that raised funds for shared causes. Ministers' unions issued statements that carried weight beyond any single group. In many counties, the practical ecumenism of teachers and mothers' boards proved more decisive than doctrinal differences on paper.

Justice at the altar rail

The altar and the bench remained two ends of one hallway. Communion reminded congregants of a table where distinctions did not rule; church discipline offered restoration pathways that civil law seldom granted. When courts failed, church processes mediated disputes with an eye to reconciliation and survival. The sacraments kept a theological claim alive:

that dignity did not depend on a deputized neighbor's whim but on a calling sealed in water and remembered in bread and cup.

Sermons for a hard century

Preaching in Reconstruction and after carried law, lament, exhortation, and consolation in unequal measures. Lessons on Proverbs and labor punctuated with warnings about debts and drink; expositions of Exodus shared pages with instructions on contract terms; Christ's Beatitudes sheltered grief and sharpened conscience. The best sermons traveled as pamphlets, taught in teachers' meetings, and re-preached in kitchens where elders rehearsed points for those who had missed the service. Style varied—lined out, extemporaneous, carefully scripted—but aim did not: to equip a people to stand.

Young men and women's auxiliaries

Auxiliaries organized youth energy into structured service: reading rooms staffed after school; errands run for elders; choirs trained sight-reading; debate clubs rehearsed arguments on questions from temperance to school funding. Young men learned to gavel; young women learned to keep the minutes and the money. When a pastor fell ill or traveled, these auxiliaries kept programs intact, proving the institution larger than any one voice.

The southern press

Denominational papers and local newsletters matured into a southern Black press capable of setting agendas and defending reputations. Columns carried serialized biographies of ministers and teachers, reports from remote circuits, school essays by prize students, and lists of subscribers that doubled as honor rolls. Editorial campaigns pressed county boards for school apportionments and scolded congregations for lateness in paying teachers. The press became both mirror and map: seeing itself in print taught a people to think regionally.

Savings, credit, and mutual aid

Small sums made durable change when disciplined across many pockets. Savings clubs bought stoves, paid insurance premiums, retired debts that threatened buildings, and kept elders off poorhouse rolls. Some churches experimented with credit unions in embryo—rotating funds that lent modest sums for tools, seeds, and start-up stalls. Repayment was enforced as much by honor and weekly visibility as by notes. These habits trained a financial literacy that would later underwrite schools, newspapers, and legal campaigns.

Civic virtue and Sabbath quiet

Sabbath order taught civic virtue. Keeping hours, dressing with care, showing patience in crowded rooms, and restraining children to careful silence were more than manners; they were practices that publicly contradicted caricature. Processions and anniversaries displayed the same discipline outdoors—lines straight, hats off at graves, banners lettered with scripture and dates. Neighbors who would never enter a church door learned something about the congregation by how it moved in public.

Toward the century's turn

By the late 1890s, these churches had become the backbone of Black civic life from tidewater to upland, from cotton belts to coalfields. They baptized in creeks and incorporated in courts; they built schools and banks, mutual-aid lodges and newspapers; they produced teachers, preachers, printers, nurses, and officeholders accustomed to minutes and midnight. They maintained hope in budgets and in benedictions, in fairs and in funerals. They taught that freedom without habit is fragile and that habit without hope is a ledger with no income. The institutions they forged would hold through retrenchment, migration, and another century's battles.

Bridge to Modern Movements

Urbanization, industrial work, and new theological currents will press these institutions to adapt again. The capacities honed under Reconstruction—education, publishing, organized benevolence, disciplined worship, and political savvy—will underwrite Social Gospel experiments, migration-era urban ministries, and later movements that insist faith must answer a city's questions as surely as it once answered the plantation's. The next chapters will follow those adaptations as congregations translate rural habits into urban networks, and Sunday discipline into weekday advocacy.

Part IV

Modern Movements

Books By Rene'

Chapter 12

The Social Gospel

Urban Ministry and the Great Migration

Between 1900 and 1950, Black congregations that had learned to organize freedom under Reconstruction retooled those practices for a new setting: tenements stacked above noisy streets, factory whistles setting hours, low wages stretched by loan sharks, influenza and tuberculosis carried by damp air, and school districts that counted Black children last when counting desks. The same habits that once built schools under steeples—minutes, ledgers, class meetings—translated into urban instruments: tenant circles, mutual-aid treasuries, visiting nurses, employment bureaus, and after-school clubs. The pulpit still called sinners home; it also read rent receipts, wage stubs, and council ordinances.

The Great Migration gave urgency and scale to that retooling. From 1916 to 1970 roughly six million Black Americans moved from the rural South to northern, midwestern, and western cities. Entire neighborhoods changed in a decade; congregations that had been regional anchors in country towns found themselves suddenly at the center of enormous urban communities. In city after city, churches became the first port of call—places where a train-tired family could find a bed for the night, a list of employers hiring that week, and a sympathetic ear that also knew how to draft a letter to a landlord or a ward alderman.[62]

Concrete examples show how deeply the social gospel took organizational form. In Harlem, Abyssinian Baptist Church under successive leaders transformed into a civic hub: beyond worship it functioned as an employment clearinghouse, a site for voter education, and a resource for new arrivals seeking lodgings and legal aid. In Chicago, Olivet Baptist—already established as one of the city's largest Black churches—expanded social services to meet urgent needs, sponsoring health clinics, relief kitchens, and evening classes that taught reading, arithmetic, and municipal procedures to adults who had never sat at a school desk.[63]

Those institutional responses were not abstract programs but life-saving practices experienced by families. Consider the experience of a representative migrating family: the Johnsons left Mississippi in 1923 with two trunks and a hope for steady work. Arriving at Chicago's Dearborn Station, they were directed by a railroad porter to a Baptist church whose basement that week hosted a reception for new arrivals. A deacon took down Mr. Johnson's skills—carpentry—steered him to a foreman who knew the church's employment list, and placed the family temporarily with a congregant who had a spare room. Mrs. Johnson found herself enrolled in an evening class on city sanitation and tenant rights while their youngest attended a Sunday afternoon club that taught counting and letter-sound drills. Within weeks the family had a steadier wage, a seat in the Sunday school, and a circulating mutual-aid ledger that would pay for a winter coat and, when tuberculosis struck a neighbor, fund a visiting nurse.

Those kinds of stories were repeated and recorded in local papers and denominational reports: congregations that had numbered in the low hundreds in rural circuits swelled to the thousands in urban parishes. Historians note that many northern churches experienced membership increases of several hundred percent in the first decades of the migration; in neighborhoods where arrivals clustered, a single sanctuary might receive waves of new pewholders so quickly that trustees had to negotiate leases for adjacent halls or schedule multiple services each Sunday. Abyssinian's growth into the thousands and Olivet's emergence as a major urban congregation were not anomalies but part of a broader pattern in which religious institutions absorbed civic functions and served as primary social-service providers long before municipal departments met the need.[64]

The social gospel in these congregations was concrete and programmatic. Employment bureaus maintained lists of employers, organized job fairs, and trained deacons to serve as intermediaries between Black job-seekers and firms that would hire them. Housing assistance ranged from short-term lodging registers to tenant unions that educated members on leases and rent strikes, and to negotiation with landlords to secure repairs. Cultural orientation classes taught migrants the mechanics of city life—maps, bus routes, factory schedules, voting registration—alongside literacy and numeracy. Health initiatives included visiting nurses funded by church collections, Sunday clinic hours to triage common illnesses, and public health campaigns that pressured city halls to improve water and sanitation. Youth programs kept working parents' children supervised, taught civic skills, and prepared a new urban generation for college and trades. Newspapers and church bulletins amplified these efforts, turning congregational minutes into community strategy.

Pastors were both preachers and civic organizers; their sermons fused abolition's moral clarity with Progressive-era tools, insisting that salvation had civic coordinates. The God who justifies also judges budgets, they proclaimed; the Christ who healed on Galilee mandated clinics on the block. Under Jim Crow's fences and disfranchisement's silences, churches built counter-publics where policy could be argued, skills learned, and action planned: vestries as classrooms, basements as council halls, newspapers as megaphones. Deacons learned to greet cousins and strangers alike, to ask about work and housing needs, to note who had a room and who needed one. Ushers learned the city's map as well as the order of service; trustees negotiated leases and charters; choirs blended southern harmonies with northern idioms to make music that bridged regions.

The result was a redefinition of ministry. Urban ministry after the Great Migration did not abandon the altar; it extended the altar into streets, hospitals, and factories. It turned sermons into civic instruction and steeples into settlement houses. In doing so, Black churches preserved community amid dislocation, converted religious conviction into durable public goods, and reshaped American cities by insisting that faith and social justice were not separate tracks but a single, urgent calling.

Without university endowments or civic charters, congregations quietly replicated settlement-house functions. Sewing circles became clothing banks; Sunshine bands kept baskets of broth and bandages ready for door-to-door visits; boys' and girls' clubs turned churchyards into safe-play zones and taught rules that transferred to work: punctuality, patience, teamwork. Lecture nights brought physicians to teach sanitation and infant care; lawyers to explain leases, warrants, and labor contracts; teachers to coach civics tests and applications; social workers to diagram how relief offices functioned and how to keep dignity intact inside them. Week by week, a parish learned to be its neighborhood's unofficial city hall.

Theology with addresses

Preaching did not thin into sentiment; it thickened into doctrine with addresses. Isaiah's call to "repair the breach" guided block-by-block campaigns for lighting and garbage pickup. Jeremiah's "seek the peace of the city" justified coalitions that ran beyond denominational lines. Jesus' healings became a syllabus for clinics; Acts' baskets and tables framed equitable distribution. Pastors taught that sanctification included budgets and calendars; that fasting should be paired with petitions; that confession demanded repairs. In Bible classes, laypeople read parables through tenant strikes and wage disputes, learning to see mammon not as abstraction but as a landlord's ledger and an employer's clock.

Print, platform, and policy

Congregational papers and denominational weeklies extended a church's voice beyond its street. Columns listed clinic hours, job openings, sanitation schedules, and council hearings; editorials pressed for playgrounds, building inspections, and school appropriations. Pastors tucked statistics into their Bibles—mortality rates, classroom ratios, rent spikes by ward—and translated numbers into moral narrative on Sunday, then back into motions for Monday's ward meetings. Letter-writing committees learned tone as a tactic, alternating indignation with precise requests; petitions carried signatures gathered at choir rehearsal and after benediction.

Temperance, Public Health, and Community Care

When historians speak of Black churches in the late nineteenth century, they most often emphasize pulpit rhetoric, education, and the struggle against legal segregation. But for many congregations, the sermon and the sickbed, the temperance pledge and the vaccination line, were inseparable. Disease — cholera, typhoid, smallpox, and the everyday ravages of poverty — shaped ministry as surely as doctrine. Churches became clinics, relief agencies, public-health outposts, and moral reformers all at once.[65]

Nowhere was that combination more visible than at Bethel AME in Baltimore. Under the long pastorate of Rev. Harvey Johnson, Bethel moved beyond Sunday exhortation to sustained public-health activism. Johnson's anti-saloon campaigns are often cited for their moral fervor, but they were also public-health strategy: saloons crowded neighborhoods, undermined household economies, and concentrated men who might delay care or spread infection. Johnson framed temperance not only as

Christian discipline but as a path to healthier families and safer homes. He preached temperance from the pulpit, organized temperance societies among congregants, and lobbied city officials for stricter licensing in Black neighborhoods — practical measures tied to the urgency of survival in crowded urban streets.

The numbers of the era made urgency impossible to ignore. In the 1890s, urban crude death rates in U.S. industrial cities commonly ranged in the mid-teens to mid-twenties per 1,000 residents, with infant mortality in the poorest neighborhoods often exceeding 150 per 1,000 live births. Nationally organized temperance groups grew rapidly during this period; by the 1890s the Woman's Christian Temperance Union and allied bodies reported membership in the low hundreds of thousands, and innumerable local and Black temperance societies counted tens of thousands more adherents. For Black pastors and lay leaders, temperance and public-health work offered measurable tools to lower those grim statistics where churches could influence them directly.

Concrete programs followed. Bethel and other AME congregations sponsored weekly clinics where volunteer nurses and trusted laywomen dispensed tonics, bandages, and basic medical advice. Where municipal services were absent or hostile, churches became the place to find a thermometer, a clean bandage, or a sympathetic ear. In some cities, pastors negotiated with local physicians to hold vaccination clinics in church basements during Sunday afternoons, permitting congregants and neighbors to receive smallpox inoculations in a familiar, non-threatening setting. Conservative estimates from contemporary reports suggest that such church-hosted clinics vaccinated hundreds in single campaigns, reaching children and adults who otherwise distrusted or could not access municipal health services.

Sister Martha Washington — a name recorded in Bethel's late-nineteenth-century minutes and preserved in later oral histories of the congregation — embodied the hands-on care that made these efforts real. A washerwoman by trade and a trusted leader among the church's women, Martha organized "neighborhood health visits." She and a small team of women carried basins, soap, and herbal remedies; they knocked on tenement doors, taught mothers how to make boiled water safe for infants, and maintained a ledger of households with fever or persistent cough. When smallpox threatened, Sister Martha organized watch groups to ensure people completed their inoculation series and to fetch food for households under quarantine. Her ledger was less a dry administrative record than a map of relationships — names, ailments, remedies, and the rhythms of neighborly care. For many residents, the church's women were the first and last line of defense against death.

Community gardens and safe-housing initiatives likewise emerged from this practical theology. Churchyards and vacant lots were turned into plots where congregants grew vegetables to combat malnutrition — a direct response to the link between diet and susceptibility to disease. Where landlords let buildings rot, some congregations brokered purchases or rented entire tenements to create safer, cleaner housing for families displaced by illness or eviction. Sorting out repairs, securing clean water, and enforcing basic sanitation became as much a pastoral responsibility as delivering sermons about sin.

Stockpiling medicine was another common and pragmatic step. Before reliable pharmacy chains existed in many Black neighborhoods, churches kept supplies on hand: castor oil, quinine, calomel, bandages, absorbent cotton, and tonics recommended by trusted physicians. Wardens and deacons learned to triage symptoms and to distinguish home-treatable ailments from those requiring urgent physician care. The church dispensary — sometimes a locked chest in the vestry, sometimes a small cabinet behind the organ — was as vital to congregants as the pulpit itself.

Education underpinned all this activity. Hygiene classes — taught in Sunday-school rooms, in sewing circles, or during evening temperance meetings — explained germy concepts in plain language: the benefits of boiling water, the importance of ventilated rooms, and techniques to avoid contaminating food. Temperance meetings reinforced these lessons by connecting alcohol use to neglect, poverty, and family breakdown; reducing drunkenness was promoted not only as moral reform, but as a practical way to keep children fed and clean and parents able to seek care quickly.

Leaders like Bishop Alexander Walters and other regional pastors reinforced these efforts at broader levels, arguing in denominational periodicals that caring for bodies was a Christian duty equal to any doctrinal exposition. Denominational conventions included reports on church clinics, on cooperative purchases of medicine, and on campaigns to open the church's doors to itinerant physicians. By the turn of the century, such reports formed a pattern: the Black church as a hybrid institution — worship center, health clinic, relief office, and civic advocate.

The convergence of temperance and public health had a moral economy: it saved wages, steadied homes, and reduced the frequency with which families fell into ruin. When a father avoided binge drinking, a household might keep enough food and rent payments to weather an illness. When a church ensured vaccination or taught hand-washing, a child might survive measles or scarlet fever that would otherwise terminate a life. These were not abstract improvements; they altered life expectancy, economic opportunity, and the fabric of neighborhood life.

Above all, these initiatives reveal a theology lived in action: faith that did not stop at prayer but moved into the gutters and tenements, into the basements where medicines were kept and into the backyards where turnips grew. Disease shaped ministry as surely as doctrine because it demanded attention now, in ways that doctrine sometimes took for granted. In the battered hymnals and ledger books of churches like Bethel AME, in Sister Martha Washington's careful entries, one finds a faith that healed, shielded, and sustained a people whose survival depended as much on clean water and steady wages as on Sunday salvation.

Temperance campaigns persisted, reframed as wage and housing protection. Every dollar kept from the saloon was a shoe, a book, a doctor's call; every payday preserved from gaming tables kept a lease intact. Savings clubs matured into rotating credit—small loans for tools, license fees, and deposits—enforced by honor and weekly visibility. Sermons paired Proverbs' warnings with rebukes aimed at employers who shaved pay, landlords who hiked rents mid-winter, and ward bosses who traded coal for votes. Deacon boards practiced quiet triage: rent for a widow this week, a dentist for a child next, a train ticket for someone being hunted.

Public health as pastoral care

Disease shaped ministry as surely as doctrine. Churches hosted visiting nurses; Sunday-school rooms doubled as vaccination clinics; basements stocked quinine, cod liver oil, later sulfa drugs and penicillin when scarce. Women's auxiliaries learned to read thermometers, spot contagion, and teach hygiene with tact; men's clubs repaired steps and windows to admit light. Funerals taught what tables could only suggest; year by year, congregations saw life expectancy rise with "clean milk" stations and sanitation drives, dip with pandemics, and rise again when discipline and medicine partnered under one roof. "Wash and pray" was not a joke; it was policy.

Youth formation and urban futures

Choirs taught breath and blend; debate clubs trained clear argument; athletics kept afternoons from corners and gangs and made teamwork a habit that later fit union halls and civic boards. When high schools opened doors wider, church tutors chased algebra and composition into evenings; when they did not, night classes filled gaps with typing, bookkeeping, and trades. Summer programs paired scripture with field trips to libraries and city offices, replacing rumor with procedure and showing young people how to read a pay stub, file a complaint, or lobby a principal. Confirmations and graduations shared pews—and speeches.

Women's leadership, expanded field

Women who had sustained benevolence through Reconstruction ran city-scale programs now. Employment registries paired newcomers to laundries, kitchens, offices, and shops; day nurseries let mothers hold jobs; maternity circles trained midwives and taught infant care; "clean block" contests turned alleys into gardens. Fairs and teas underwrote scholarships; civic clubs born in vestries visited school boards and health commissioners; deaconess orders professionalized care with uniforms, training courses, and reports that read like municipal case files. When men occupied pulpits and chaired boards, women often owned the calendar—and the results.

Polity under pressure

Urban scale stressed denominational systems. Bishops and associations tasked pastors with budgets and payrolls that rivaled small firms; trustees managed mortgages indexed to city land values; superintendents coordinated Sunday schools with hundreds enrolled. Disputes multiplied—music budgets, building plans, liturgical taste, pastoral tenure—and so did procedural skill: bylaws revised, audits published, elections run cleanly, grievances channeled through committees that preferred reconciliation to rupture. The church was a civics school because it practiced civics every week.

The southern wing adapts

In southern cities, ministry adapted to surveillance. Clinics hid in plain sight as "aid societies;" literacy classes ran under "Bible study;" employment bureaus wore the label "men's clubs." Pastors translated caution into continuity—knowing which officer would sign a permit, which doctor would sign a certificate, which editor would print a meeting notice without naming the organizer. The same ledger that tracked communion cups counted train tickets north for those newly threatened. Suitcases under choir robes were not dramatic symbols; they were contingency plans.

Labor, strikes, and the pulpit

Industrial injuries and wage cuts pushed churches into labor's grammar. Pastors blessed picket lines and set conditions—no drinking, no stones; deacons posted bail; women's boards fed strikers' children; lecture nights taught blacklists and injunctions, "company scrip" and "closed shop." Not every strike drew pulpit support; prudence argued with principle in vestries late into nights. But a generation learned the structure of grievance and negotiation, the difference between rhetoric and leverage, and the moral stakes of a pay envelope.

Riots, law, and resilience

Riots in northern and border cities taught congregations to plan for sudden flights, legal defense, and rebuilding. Trustee boards compiled inventories and insured what could be insured; lawyers drafted claims and coordinated affidavits; pastors brokered truces with precinct captains when possible and denounced dereliction when necessary. After violence, sanctuaries held mass meetings where lament and resolve shared time: committees tracked arrests, raised funds, repaired porches, petitioned grand juries, and escorted children back to school past corners where glass still crunched. Hymns steadied hands that still trembled.

Ecumenism and coalitions

Competition bent to coalition when city halls stalled. Ministers' unions convened across denominational lines; combined choirs raised funds for clinics and playgrounds; women's councils standardized school-lunch menus and textbook lists. Joint statements pressed mayors for police reform, sanitation schedules, fair hiring for public works, and appointments of Black nurses and teachers. Coalition was ritual—rotating host pulpits, shared offering plates, combined committees—and craft—shared talking points, press deadlines, disciplined follow-up.

Foreign missions and a widened lens

Foreign missions absorbed social-gospel methods as nurses, teachers, and pastors linked evangelism with clinics, schools, and agricultural training. Reports from West Africa and the Caribbean returned with a widened lens: empire critiqued, Pan-African ties named, anticolonial hopes taught in Sunday schools. A child who learned to trace rivers in a mission atlas learned to trace a local sewer map; a congregation that prayed for a far-off clinic insisted on one in its own ward. "To the ends of the earth" and "to the end of the block" were bound by the same habit.

Music, media, and message

Hymnals updated; gospel choirs rose; quartets toured circuits that doubled as information networks. Radio microphones in the 1930s carried sermons beyond stained glass, and with them appeals for blood drives, polio vaccinations, and strike funds. Print shops in basements set tracts on housing covenants and police powers; mimeographs and offset presses multiplied flyers by the hundreds in hours. The sound of the social gospel was part doxology, part bulletin; its look was part broadside, part Sunday program.

Depression, relief, and federal partnership

The Great Depression made social work a survival skill. Soup kettles stretched; clothing banks expanded; shutoff funds kept water and heat in place; job clubs shared leads and coached interviews. Churches partnered with relief offices and later with federal programs, then critiqued gaps: insisting that aid respect dignity, that work programs hire Black labor at scale, and that home-mortgage supports reach neighborhoods historically starved of credit. Pastors learned eligibility charts; secretaries learned forms; treasurers kept parallel ledgers—one for offerings, one for reimbursements.

Theological debates at street level

Activism drew critique: some feared "politics in the pulpit," others preferred a narrower pietism, still others worried about denominational backlash. Social gospel pastors paced change, built broad consent, published budgets and outcomes, and kept worship beautiful enough that even critics stayed for the benediction. The deepest debates were theological: Kingdom-now versus patience; cross as moral influence versus cross as solidarity with the crucified; "render to Caesar" as limit versus as leverage. Study circles read scripture alongside pamphlets, rehearsing arguments that would later fill mass meetings.

Youth to leadership

By midcentury, youth trained in church gyms, libraries, choirs, and debate clubs stepped into pulpits, school boards, unions, newsrooms, and health departments. Their administrative fluency—scheduling, chairing meetings, publishing notices, auditing funds—translated into civic leadership. They had learned to argue without breaking fellowship, to balance prudence and courage, and to make plans that could be prayed and executed. When the next phase demanded marshals, they were ready; when carpools needed dispatchers, they already owned maps; when a negotiating committee needed a chair, they knew the gavel's weight.

Women's Social Gospel Leadership

If the building campaigns, pledge cards, and burned mortgages were the public face of Black congregational life, the quieter axis of daily care—education, health, work, and mutual aid—was run by women whose labors turned charity into durable institutions. Their work was not secondary; it was structural. Women read the neighborhood before the men read a brief; they learned what a family needed by keeping the calendar of births, wash days, sewing bees, and funerals. When men occupied formal pulpits and presidencies, women often owned the calendar—and the results.

Nannie Helen Burroughs offers the clearest portrait of that ownership turned into institutional form. In 1909, in a modest building on the edge of Washington, D.C., she founded the National Training School for Women and Girls. It was not simply a charity or an industrial school in the old sense; it was an intentional social-gospel project aimed at economic self-sufficiency, moral formation, and civic responsibility. Burroughs insisted that Black women should learn bookkeeping, sewing, public speaking, and pedagogy—skills that translated into work and authority. Her commencements were fundraising events, pedagogical spectacles, and political statements: graduates left with diplomas and with networks that fed into church auxiliaries, day nurseries, and employment registries. The school's ledger reads like a map of Black women's social economy—tuition paid in cash and in domestic labor, gifts of fabric for the sewing room, subscriptions raised by name and by prayer.[66]

That combination of pedagogy and parish organizing was common. In Philadelphia, Mrs. Sarah Mapps Douglass—the teacher, abolitionist, and tireless organizer—turned a parlor meeting into a city-wide women's mission society. The story has a domestic intimacy that reveals how public institutions were born. Douglass convened a handful of women, unfolded a subscription list on the dining table, and asked who among them would visit the sick, teach a night school, or petition a city inspector about a rowhouse deemed uninhabitable. They sewed, baked, and tabulated pledges in the same hands that taught the alphabet and led prayer. Within months, that society was running day schools for girls, organizing weekly soup kitchens, and establishing a maternity circle that connected expectant mothers to midwives and to a rotating fund for layette needs. Douglass's minutes read like sermons and municipal reports: moral exhortation fused with neighborhood statistics and an eye toward sustaining resources.

The scale of this work is easier to see when we look at membership lists and bank accounts. Across denominations, women's auxiliaries multiplied in the late nineteenth and early twentieth centuries. Where once a single missionary society met in a church basement, by the 1910s auxiliary meetings filled parlors, lecture halls, and hotel ballrooms. Contemporary denominational reports show membership swelling from the low thousands in the postbellum decades to the tens of thousands—locally and nationally—by the 1910s and 1920s. A small-town women's auxiliary might raise $200 to $500 a year—enough to keep a day nursery open through the winter—while larger urban federations, through annual bazaars and mother's day drives, aggregated sums in the thousands. National campaigns—often joint ventures among mission societies, temperance clubs, and the National Association of Colored Women's Clubs—could bring collections into five figures, underwriting settlement houses, scholarship funds, and hospital wards. Those numbers were not dry tallies; they were lifelines: the dollars paid nurses' wages, bought coal, and kept the lights on in maternity centers during epidemics.

The programs these women built were both pragmatic and visionary. Settlement houses run by Black women—less grand in architecture than white counterparts but no less formidable in impact—served as neighborhood hubs: they housed vocational classes, child care, and health educa-tion. Vocational training explicitly linked to church auxiliaries prepared girls and young women for remunerative work as dressmakers, teachers, domestic managers, and clerical workers. Employment registries, main-tained by women's societies, functioned as proto-placement bureaus: a register listed seamstresses, cooks, laundresses, and nursemaids, matching names to employers and collecting small fees that underwrote the registry's office and the woman who kept it. These registries were practical tools for upward mobility; they reduced the friction between skill and paid work.[67]

Maternity circles and maternal health initiatives were another arena where women converted communal care into institutional power. Moth-ers' clubs pooled money to hire midwives, purchased infant formula and linens, and ran postpartum visiting programs that taught hygiene and breastfeeding—or, in the language of the day, "domestic science." Day nurseries—hourly, affordable child care centers—let mothers go out to work, attend classes at the training school, or recover from illness without surrendering their employment. In many cities, the nursery was the only safe space for children whose mothers labored in factories and laundries. The cumulative effect was measurable: infant-feeding programs and visit-ing nurses reduced local infant mortality; vocational instruction increased women's wages; employment registries shortened the interval between job loss and reemployment.[68]

Civic clubs provided the connective tissue between church work and public advocacy. Clubwomen organized campaigns for sanitation, school reform, playgrounds, and suffrage. They produced petitions, hosted can-didates, and collected data—surveys of tenement conditions, lists of un-licensed boarding houses, and tabulations of working hours. The Na-tional Association of Colored Women's Clubs, with leaders such as Mary Church Terrell, converted localized charity into a platform for national re-form, bringing maternal health and anti-lynching advocacy into the main-stream of civic discourse. At the local level, smaller civic clubs lily-padded into municipal boards, influencing school hiring and municipal nursing services.

Personal stories illuminate how these programs functioned. A seamstress in Atlanta might learn bookkeeping at a Burroughs-style school, find work through an employment registry, place her toddler in a day nursery three blocks from church, and serve on the maternity circle that supported a neighbor after childbirth. That one woman's week—classes on Monday, paid work Tuesday through Thursday, club meeting Friday—shows how the calendar of women's commitments stitched together economic survival and public improvement. Women learned to manage time and to measure results: attendance lists, subscription tallies, and fundraising thermometers were tools of accountability as well as motivation. Where a pastor announced needs from the pulpit, the women's committee met the next day and made the plan.

The language of stewardship—the doxologies for paid-off notes and the collective sigh for a new organ—meets a different vocabulary in women's hands: ledgers of hours given, of babies placed in nurseries, of women taught to read temperate pedigrees. Their worship was organizational as much as liturgical. Their victories were often small—reopening a nursery after a winter of closures, keeping a maternity nurse on retainer during an influenza season—but cumulatively they altered life chances for generations.

That practical liturgy mattered because it redistributed power. Even when denominational structures placed men in visible offices, women's auxiliaries set agendas, mobilized resources, and sustained daily charity. They owned the calendar—and when the calendar produced clean water, shorter working hours for girls, and a trained midwife on call, they also owned the results.

Respectability and its limits

Respectability—dress, diction, punctuality, audited accounts—opened doors to meetings and tempered bias in courts, but it could be a trap if mistaken for justice. Churches learned to deploy it as strategy while teaching youth to see its limits: that a pressed suit might win a hearing but would not by itself change a hiring list; that a spotless ledger might protect a charter but would not desegregate a ward. The dance between optics and structural change became part of the curriculum.

Cemeteries, clinics, and continuity

The social gospel ran from cradle to grave in practical lines: maternity circles to midwives; well-baby clinics to school health checks; workmen's comp guidance to hospital chaplaincy; funerals that dignified lives the city barely noticed. Cemeteries organized by churches extended the ethic: clean paths, readable stones, flowers planted by youth groups. Remembering names did more than console; it taught continuity—the sense that the work outlasts the worker and requires the next set of hands.

Art, culture, and civic stage

Sanctuaries became stages for more than sermons: plays on tenant rights, pageants of emancipation, concerts that raised funds and spirits. Painters hung exhibits in fellowship halls; poets read on Friday nights; photographers documented "before and after" blocks where cleanups and gardens reset a street's mood. Culture was not an add-on; it was a form of claim-staking: a public beauty that contradicted slum narratives and taught children to take care because something lovely had been entrusted to them.

Building Institutions: Schools, Banks, and Community Centers

If freedom meant more than the absence of chains, Black communities after emancipation built the tangible ladders that made possibility real. Education, credit, and common space were not afterthoughts; they were the essential infrastructure of survival and ascent. Against the deliberate neglect and active hostility of Jim Crow, churches, mutual aid lodges, benevolent societies, and a new generation of Black educators and entrepreneurs set up schools, banks, and community centers that taught skills, pooled capital, and cultivated civic life. Those institutions — Spelman College and Hampton Institute among them, Atlanta Life Insurance Company, scores of Black-run banks, YMCA/YWCA branches and church-sponsored credit unions — became the scaffolding on which families climbed.

Schools were the most immediate and visible lever. In towns and rural counties across the South, formerly enslaved people and their descendants converted one-room spaces into classrooms, then expanded into normal schools and colleges. Hampton Institute (founded 1868) and Spelman College (founded 1881) are emblematic. Hampton trained teachers and industrial workers for the new economy; Spelman became a center for Black women's higher learning and leadership. In the classrooms labeled "Normal" — shorthand for teacher training — students learned pedagogy, child psychology, and the day-to-day craft of schooling. Alongside reading, arithmetic, and Bible study, schools offered construction, carpentry, and domestic science; they taught stenography and bookkeeping; they prepared students for college entrance exams. These were not merely academic exercises. A graduate who could teach, type, or manage school records could command steady wages in a precarious labor market and in turn support a family, buy a home, and participate in civic life.

Consider the experience of students at Hampton: early mornings in the dormitory, a regimen that combined classical study with practical labor on the farm and in the print shop. A young woman might spend the morning in a Normal class learning lesson plans and child development, the afternoon world in a shorthand and stenography course that would prepare her to work in an office, and the evening studying algebra or rhetoric. Those combinations — literacy plus vocational dexterity — were strategic. They created mobility not only for individuals but for communities hungry for reliable teachers, clerks, and small-business managers.

Education alone could not finance families or enterprises. That role fell to a parallel creation of economic institutions. Atlanta Life Insurance Company, founded in 1905 by Alonzo Herndon, is one well-known exemplar: an insurance firm that sold policies to Black clients who otherwise had little protection against sickness, accident, or death. Insurance payments, regular premiums, and the discipline of saving translated into economic resilience. Church-sponsored credit unions and mutual aid societies did the same work on a community scale. In many neighborhoods, congregations ran small savings-and-loan operations that accepted modest deposits, issued micro-loans for head-of-household emergencies, or helped a seamstress or barber expand a shop. Families who used these credit unions could, for the first time, finance home repairs, buy furniture, or put a child through normal school — acts that built wealth slowly but durably.

We should name the organizations and the scale at which they operated. Between Reconstruction and the eve of World War II, Black communities established thousands of schools and hundreds of community centers; dozens of Black-owned banks and insurance companies emerged in cities and regional centers. Mutual aid lodges and benevolent societies enrolled memberships often in the hundreds and, in major urban areas, sometimes into the thousands. The Independent Order of St. Luke, for instance, moved from fraternal ritual into commercial and financial activity under leaders who understood that pooled membership meant pooled capital. Maggie L. Walker's St. Luke Penny Savings Bank (founded in 1903) is one of the clearest demonstrations of the leap from club to bank. These figures are not abstractions: each schoolhouse, each branch office, each YMCA or YWCA meant one more place where literacy took root, where savings accumulated, and where social networks deepened.

Community centers — especially Black branches of the YMCA and YWCA — served complementary roles. In segregated cities the "colored" YMCA/YWCA branches were often the only places young people could access gymnasiums, reading rooms, vocational classes, and quiet study halls. Many branches offered stenography and secretarial courses targeted to women, plumbing and carpentry workshops for young men, and evening classes in civics and history that fed leadership pipelines for churches and local politics. These spaces were also meeting places for political organizing, voter education, and legal aid in an era when many public institutions were closed to Black citizens.

The economic data embedded in these institutions tell a story of self-help and mutuality. Church-sponsored business development — from funeral homes and boardinghouses to insurance agencies and bakeries — was often financed on a rotating-credit or pooled-membership basis. Mutual aid societies guaranteed that members could pay for funerals and short-term illness; the regular dues of hundreds of members became a predictable float for small loans. In cities with larger Black populations, such collective capital helped seed real estate investment and storefront enterprises, sustaining a Black middle class even when mainstream banks excluded them. The consequence was measurable: neighborhoods with active institutional infrastructures retained more stable property ownership, had higher rates of school attendance, and produced a disproportionate share of teachers, nurses, and clerical workers.

The long-term impact of these intertwined institutions cannot be overstated. Through the Jim Crow decades, they provided the continuity of schooling, credit, and communal life. Schools produced the teachers who kept literacy and civic knowledge alive; banks and insurance companies made possible the accumulation and transfer of modest wealth; community centers kept young people engaged and trained professionals for the expanding bureaucratic workplaces of the 20th century. In times of violence and legal disenfranchisement, churches and lodges were often the only safe havens from which coordinated responses — boycotts, legal funds, and mass meetings — could be organized.

Perhaps the most important measure of success is generational. The stenographer trained in a YMCA evening class could become the office manager who hired others; the teacher trained in a Normal department could educate the next generation of lawyers and doctors; the homeowner who bought a property with a church-backed loan could pass it to children who attended Spelman or Hampton. These institutional ladders created cumulative advantage in a society designed to deny it.

What emerges from these histories is not romanticized self-sufficiency but a deliberate, communal strategy. Black Americans built buffers and bridges: schools to teach and certify talent, banks and insurance firms to retain and deploy capital, and community centers to host the social and civic life necessary for collective advancement. They were, in short, builders of institutions — practical, visionary, and enduring — that sustained communities through adversity and laid the groundwork for future claims to equality.

From Sabbath-school primers to high-school scholarships to adult night schools, education ladders multiplied under steeples. "Normal" classes trained teachers for weekday schools; stenography and bookkeeping fed graduates into offices; trade classes introduced carpentry, plumbing, and electrical basics. College-bound students found mentors who explained applications, entrance exams, and how to ride a train to a campus that might be the first view of lawns kept by somebody else's budget. Every diploma returned to the pulpit for a blessing; every failure returned to a pew for another try.

Budgets, audits, and trust

Trust traveled on paper and habit. Annual reports listed receipts and disbursements line by line; independent auditors signed their names; budgets were posted on bulletin boards; collections for special purposes were counted by rotating teams. These practices answered slander, reassured donors, and taught youth that honesty is an institutional discipline, not a mood. When thefts occurred, discipline was firm and private; when rumors spread, facts were printed.

Crisis choreography

Fire, flood, epidemic, riot—crises rehearsed choreography. An usher's tap meant a deacon at the side door; a bell's pattern meant volunteers to the basement; a whispered name meant a doctor summoned without lights. Lists were kept: who had keys, who had cars, who could be trusted with cash, who could be trusted with children. After-action reports were real: trustees revised procedures, pastors adjusted phrases, nurses updated kits. The point was not drama; it was survival with dignity.

The long apprenticeship to movement

By 1950, the Black social gospel had produced an infrastructure of leaders, habits, and tools: clinics and choirs, newspapers and nurseries, budget committees and bailout funds, ushers who could move a crowd and treasurers who could stretch a coin. It had weathered migration, riot, pandemic, Depression, and everyday municipal indifference. It argued theology with addresses and turned addresses into theology. When lightning struck a southern city in December 1955, the people who caught it had already been practicing—with clipboards, ladles, songbooks, and ledgers—for two generations.

The pulpit cadence that steadied crowded tenements will command mass meetings; ushers' crowd skills will become march marshaling; deacons' bail funds will turn into legal defenses; the hymn that soothed mothers will become the soundtrack of a movement aimed not just at relief, but at law, custom, and conscience across a nation.

Chapter 13

The Church Militant

A movement with a steeple

Between 1950 and 1970, the Southern freedom struggle moved on church calendars, in church basements, and under church rafters. Sanctuaries became strategy rooms where ushers learned to marshal marches, deacons learned bail procedures, and choirs learned how to hold a crowd's breath through fear. Sunday rhythms—call and response, scripture and exhortation—translated into mass-meeting cadence that instructed, steadied, and sent people back into streets where law, custom, and violence were joined. The church did not watch the movement; it housed it, disciplined it, and gave it a language that could say "we" when "I" might run.[69]

Old habits turned to tactics

What Reconstruction taught in minutes and ledgers matured into logistics fit for confrontation. The skills of collecting and auditing became fund drives for court costs. The habit of punctuality became march timetables that beat police ambush by fifteen minutes. The practice of testimony became training for affidavits and press interviews. Prayer lists became emergency contact rosters. Women's boards that once managed coal and milk now managed child care for arrested parents, food lines for walkers, and supply chains for boycotts measured in months. The ordinary work of church life proved to be a long apprenticeship in nonviolent discipline.

Pulpits as command posts

Pastors turned platforms into control centers. They explained injunctions, arrests, bond amounts, and the rules of picket lines: no taunting, no return blows, keep lines straight, keep songs steady. They mediated between generational styles—older deacons wary of jail, students eager to go—and transformed that tension into a division of labor: elders held the building, youth took the first blows, everyone met for prayer. Sermons named targets—lunch counters, buses, registrars' offices—without naming names that would invite a night's visit. In Sunday clothes and weekday voices, clergy became tacticians whose weapon was instruction made sacred by the call to love.

Training for nonviolence

Nonviolence did not come naturally; it was taught. Church classrooms turned into workshops where students and elders took turns playing attacker and attacked, where insults were shouted, drinks poured, shoves given, and the discipline of stillness practiced until muscles remembered how not to answer. Role-plays set rules: protect the head, cover another's back, do not break line to rescue a friend if that breaks the tactic, memorize bail procedures, keep a hymn ready as a breathing exercise. Deacons who had once enforced quiet in pews now enforced composure in doorways surrounded by jeers, and ushers who had directed aisles now learned to manage sidewalks.[70]

Songs that held courage

Music turned fear into forward motion. Hymns and spirituals—sung in four parts, lined out when necessary—became the oxygen of meetings and marches. "Guide Me, O Thou Great Jehovah" steadied feet; "Ain't Gonna Let Nobody Turn Me Around" gave the crowd a spine; "We Shall Overcome" reset hearts to the long beat, reminding a people that endurance is tempo. Choir directors arranged songs to alternate lament and resolve; soloists timed crescendos to the moment a sheriff entered the back; youth choirs pitched refrains at a register that cut through chant and siren. A movement that needed breath found it in song.[71]

Women's engines of the movement

Women ran the gears that kept motion smooth. They staffed phone trees, printed flyers, filed membership rolls that doubled as emergency lists, cooked for a hundred after mass meetings, and pressed shirts for court days. They chaired committees that decided which family got a bag of groceries and which landlord needed a call. They kept ledgers accurate enough to persuade a skeptical judge and kind enough to remember a child's new shoes. When the platform drew male voices, the calendar and the checkbook bore women's names. Their leadership was rarely ceremonial and often decisive.

Youth energy and church discipline

Student energy drove risk; church discipline kept it from burning itself up. College chapels hosted night-by-night trainings; Sunday schools became weeknight strategy pods; youth choirs doubled as picket squads. The sanctuary gave students moral cover, institutional density, and a communications hub reachable by family and press. Elders taught students to pace themselves: to rotate arrests, to write phone numbers on wrists, to accept that a day in jail might be a tactic rather than a catastrophe. Students taught elders to escalate appropriately: a sit-in here, a kneel-in there, a boycott where money could speak.

Law, affidavits, and bail

The church became a legal workshop. Deacons learned to spot a lawful order from a bluff, to note badge numbers without staring, to file affidavits that held up in court. Treasurers mastered bond schedules and bail procedures; secretaries kept arrest logs with times, charges, and jail locations; pastors learned which county clerks would take a midnight call. Fundraising made law practical: usher-stored coins and widow-given dollars turned into release from a cell; special offerings on a Sunday paid for injunction challenges on a Monday. Arrest-night prayers shared space with lists of names that had to be called.[72]

Countering fear and fatigue

Mass meetings were not rallies for their own sake; they were spiritual technologies designed to counter exhaustion and terror. The order of service was a tactic: long singing until shoulders dropped; a testimony to insert narrative into rumor; the sermon that rehearsed history, named law, and dignified the next day's ordinary courage; the offering that allowed those without wages to buy their children's safety with a coin; the benediction that sent a crowd out as a cohort. In parking lots after, men loaned cars, women loaned coats, youths walked elders to corners where hecklers waited. Courage learned repetition.

Surveillance and counter-surveillance

Sanctuaries did not shield eyes and ears. Informers attended and took notes; phones clicked; cars circled. Churches adapted: they compartmentalized plans, rehearsed decoy routes, assigned lookouts who knew uniforms by cut and unmarked cars by habit. A meeting might be public and the tactic inside it private; a press release spoke loud while the real work moved quiet. The ethics were not romantic; they were pastoral: to protect the weak while exposing injustice, to confuse agents bent on harm while clarifying purpose to a people.

Violence and the holy ground

Bombings turned pews into splinters; bullets ricocheted off stained glass; gasoline turned hymnals to ash. After blasts, congregations gathered on the lawn, counted heads, and sang while smoke still rose. Clean-up crews swept glass without ceremony; trustees called insurers and cousins with hammers; pastors wrote statements that refused despair and refused to deny grief. Funerals for victims of racial terror became the movement's high sacraments: eulogies that joined lament to charge, processions that turned streets into altars, vows not to forget tied to concrete plans to move the next petition, the next boycott, the next march.[73]

Boycott logic and church geography

Boycotts worked because churches already knew how to map neighborhoods and keep schedules. Car-pool dispatchers used pew charts repurposed; mechanics in congregations kept station wagons running; nursery workers watched toddlers while mothers walked; deacons politely confronted neighbors crossing lines, offering rides to shoppers tempted by convenience. Sunday from pulpits drilled weekday routes ("If anyone needs a lift from the corner of ..."), and Wednesday night prayers became check-ins on blisters and tips for grease-stained hands. The boycott was part liturgy, part logistics.

Voter registration as catechism

Registration drives borrowed church routines and language. Bible-study times became training slots for form-filling; catechism became quiz prep for "literacy" tests designed to fail; altar calls became sign-ups for rides to registrar offices. Ushers turned into line marshals; choir members sang softly in hallways where hours stretched; pastors prepared affidavits on birth dates from family Bibles. When sheriffs blocked doors, the congregation that had practiced patience in pews practiced patience on courthouse steps. Baptism and ballot shared one argument: a human being has a name, a witness, and a right to be counted.

Coalitions across the aisle

The movement's church power multiplied in coalition. Ministers' unions offered rotating pulpits for mass meetings, shared offering plates for shared jails, and coordinated calendars that reduced burnout. Women's councils synchronized school-lunch campaigns and textbook petitions. White allies in pulpits and pews, few but real, opened spaces and wrote editorials, while Jewish and Catholic partners offered legal aid and public cover. Coalitions required habit—time limits honored, speaking orders kept, public disagreements contained. The discipline that kept a choir in time kept a coalition intact.

Media and the moral stage

Churches understood the camera as courtroom. Mass meetings were staged for witness: packed pews, elevated pulpits, choirs in robes, a sequence of speakers that built an arc. Press tables were treated like communion rails—approached with reverence, fed with clean copy, protected from rumor. Photographers were given angles; radio mics were instructed not to overmodulate; newspaper deadlines were met. This was not vanity; it was sacred theater for a secular jury, inviting a nation to see what the city would not show itself.

Generational tension and the shared task

Disagreement was an engine, not a break. Students demanded immediacy; elders demanded strategy. Pulpits hosted both: one night a college choir singing with clenched hands; another, a senior deacon describing a white employer's soft-spoken cruelty. The church turned this into pedagogy: teach the long arc and the short lever, the day-by-day grinding and the lightning strike. Meetings closed with hymns not to hush debate but to place it inside a covenant that would hold longer than a headline.

Theology sharpened in practice

Doctrine was forged under pressure. Sermons parsed the Sermon on the Mount not as passivity but as disciplined pressure: turn the other cheek as refusal to let an enemy choose the terms of encounter; love enemies as requirement to see beyond this officer to the order that made him; prayer as form of breath control in a jail where air tastes of bleach and fear. Exodus read as both a map and a warning: seas do not part without long marches; deserts test resolve; quails do not fatten complainers. The Lord's Supper became a weekly reminder that a table makes kin of unlikely neighbors, that a body broken can be a body reborn.

The pastor as field commander

Pastoral work became crisis management. A day's list read like triage: bail two students; visit a mother whose son lost teeth to a deputy's ring; negotiate a permit; call a sympathetic reporter; meet a donor; meet a lawyer; write a statement; answer a death threat; preside at Bible study; sleep four hours. The skill set expanded: legal vocabulary, press timing, de-escalation tactics, and the old arts of hospital visits and funerals. The burden was mortal; the calling, unromantic. Many burned out; some broke; others found strange strength in the crowd's song and the widow's mite.

Men's clubs, boys' brigades, and marshals

The same groups that once planned fish fries and baseball leagues now trained march marshals. They learned hand signals, column spacing, and how to turn a hundred bodies around without panic when a road blocked. They identified steady men to walk near hotheads; they assigned veterans to edges; they studied maps and estimated arrival times for cameras. A quiet man with a whistle could preserve a march when violence tempted chaos.

Sacrament and strategy in one house

The movement's power came from keeping what seemed opposite in one house: sacrament and strategy, worship and planning, lament and logistics. A sanctuary held the contradictions without shattering: here, a table set for the meek; there, a chalkboard diagramming how to break a police encirclement; here, a prayer for the jailer's child; there, a list of badge numbers to give a lawyer. The unity was not rhetorical; it was spatial and temporal. People stood where they had been married to hear how to face a dog; they sang where they had buried a child to learn the law's next trap.

Setbacks, schisms, and the long view

Not every campaign won; not every coalition held. Injunctions bit; arrests scattered; a bomb shook resolve; a compromise soured in the mouth. Churches responded with their oldest move: they kept meeting. They read minutes after defeats; they balanced books after fines; they replaced windows and restarted choirs. When schisms came—over tactics, over pace, over pride—new congregations planted down the street, singing the same songs and adopting the same minutes they had left. The long view was embodied: next Sunday comes, and with it the next chance to gather breath.

The rural circuit and the hard road

Outside cities, rural churches held quieter, no less dangerous lines: registration by kitchen light; classes in schoolhouses after dusk; services interrupted by headlights and questions. Pastors worked by day in fields and by night in jail corridors. A congregation that had nothing to spare still found coins for a neighbor's fine. Travel was the enemy; distances too long to walk, cars too few, tires too bald. Yet the circuit held because the habit held: schedule, sing, pass the hat, try again.

Northern air, southern roots

Movement needed money and media; churches sent both north. Delegations traveled to pulpits that answered with offerings, press contacts, and volunteer lawyers. The old migration routes ran in reverse: a deacon's son from Detroit learned to run a sound system; a choir from Chicago lifted a meeting in a mill town; a doctor from Boston answered a midnight call. The South held the frontline; the North kept the rear supplied. The map looked like a web, its nodes marked by steeples.

Children watching, children leading

Children sat on laps at mass meetings, counted the number of hymns before bedtime, and learned to clap on the two and the four. They memorized verse and verse-turned-slogan; they watched parents leave for jail with a prayer and a sandwich; they learned that fear can be breathed through and that tired feet can keep time if a song is strong. In some towns, they marched first because city fathers misjudged their courage. The movement's future leaders learned to speak in Sunday-school circles and at microphones that stood taller than they were.

From pulpit to platform

By the late 1960s, the church's leaders stood on bigger stages: at podiums on national malls, at committee tables where legislation took shape, in studios where interviews could slip into stump speeches. The skills had been honed in smaller rooms: know the audience, don't waste a minute, cite scripture that makes sense to believers and skeptics, tell a story that ties a bill number to a grandmother's kitchen. Even as national attention grew, home calendars still ruled: funerals on Friday, weddings on Saturday, sermon on Sunday, meeting on Monday.

A movement that prayed with calloused hands

The Church Militant prayed with calloused hands and tired throats. It believed that love could be organized, that hope could be scheduled, that mercy could be marched. It treated the city as a parish and the law as a field to be harvested for justice. It raised offerings that turned into shoes and subpoenas, into bus tires and broadcast airtime. It baptized conviction in cold water and confirmed it in hot streets. And it taught a nation to sing.

The campaigns won laws and shifted the nation's conscience, but victories opened questions the street alone could not settle. The next phase presses theology to speak explicitly about power, class, gender, and the meaning of Blackness before God and neighbor. Out of pulpits and seminaries will come a body of thought that names liberation not only as practice but as doctrine—and that argues, sometimes fiercely, over how the church should wield its hard-won authority.

Chapter 14

Liberation Theology

A new language for old work

In the wake of mass meetings and municipal fights, congregations and classrooms began to ask for a grammar that could name what they already practiced: a gospel that judged structures, not only souls; a cross that broke chains, not only hearts; a resurrection that stood the poor upright in courtrooms and clinics. Between 1960 and 1990, a body of thought took shape across pulpits and seminaries that called itself liberation theology, insisting that God's preferential concern for the oppressed was not a sentiment but a method. The same elders who had planned boycotts now listened to lectures that explained why those boycotts were theology in action; the same students who had trained for sit-ins now read books that sounded like their own lives set to argument.

Sources and streams

Liberation theology did not arrive as a single river. It flowed through multiple channels that converged: Latin American Catholic reflections foregrounding the poor and base communities; Black theology in the United States naming God's solidarity with Black people under white supremacy; Womanist theology insisting that Black women's experiences were not footnotes but a primary text; Asian and African voices adapting the same insistence to caste, dictatorial power, and neocolonial markets. In each stream, the vow was similar: read scripture with those who bear the heaviest burdens; treat experience not as anecdote but as a laboratory where doctrine is tested; and measure claims by their effect on the least protected.[74]

From street to syllabus

The church had long practiced what movement demanded—funds collected, calendars kept, coalitions maintained—but now faculty and pastors laid those practices alongside scripture and tradition and asked what they implied for Christology, ecclesiology, and ethics. Courses with titles like "Church and Social Change," "Theology and the City," and "The Bible and the Poor" migrated from extension programs to core curricula. Internships paired classroom exegesis with hospital chaplaincy, tenant advocacy, prison Bible study, and clinic support. Evaluations graded not only papers, but the capacity to organize a meeting and deliver a report that told truth without exposing the vulnerable.

Reading the Bible from below

Exegesis changed posture. Instead of asking what a text meant in a study alone, interpreters took questions from kitchens, union halls, hospital wards, and block associations. Exodus became a manual for people who knew Pharaoh by another name; the prophets sounded like nightly news; the Gospels read as a dossier on a man who touched untouchables and crossed lines drawn to keep power stable. Paul's letters were re-examined with Roman law and household hierarchies in view, not to sanctify subordination, but to expose strategy: how communities endured within structures they could not yet overturn while training to resist them. The hermeneutical circle—experience to text, text to experience—was not a slogan but a habit that set the week's reading against the week's headlines.

Sin and structures

Doctrine stretched. Sin, once taught primarily as personal failure, was named also as architecture: schools funded to fail some children, hospitals priced to exclude some bodies, neighborhoods redlined into sickness and shortened lives. Repentance was not merely confession and a new will; it was policy and repair: budget lines, ordinances, and contracts rewritten to cease harm and begin restitution. Salvation, correspondingly, reached wider: not a ticket out, but a life within—work with dignity, home with safety, clinic without humiliation, law without predation. The shift did not erase personal piety; it anchored it in common life where a neighbor's need made the believer's calendar.

Christ and the crucified of history

Christology found a sharper edge. To confess Christ crucified was to recognize him among people publicly shamed, economically stripped, and legally hunted; to confess him risen was to trust that those people's lives were not doomed to repetition of injury. A theology that stayed on Golgotha too long excused despair; a theology that rushed to Easter denied the cost. Sermons learned to keep both truths in the same paragraph: the reality of wounds and the refusal to cede the future to those who inflicted them. Pastoral care drew energy from that pairing, offering comfort without anesthetic and hope without fantasy.

Church as base community

Parish life adapted. The small group—long familiar in class meetings and prayer circles—was now tasked explicitly with reading the Bible against the neighborhood's needs, then carrying plans back to trustees and councils. A "base community" could be a few apartments on one floor, a row of houses on a block, a circle of nurses at a hospital, a group of bus drivers on a route. Their work: study, mutual aid, and targeted action small enough to succeed and large enough to teach skills transferrable to bigger fights. Minutes recorded victories and failures; testimonies rehearsed lessons learned; and the pulpit summarized patterns so more circles could replicate them.

Liturgy and life

Worship bore the marks of new purpose. Prayers named evictions and indictments; intercessions listed hospitals and schools by name; confession expanded to include silence in the face of neighbors' harm; thanksgiving counted policy changes alongside recoveries from illness. Music carried lament and fight in the same service—psalms that grieved violence and songs that stiffened spines. The Eucharist, long understood as communion with God and one another, was preached as a refusal of stratification: one bread, one cup, one table where the city's maps of better and worse addresses were suspended.

Critique and communion

Liberation theology drew critique from several directions. Some feared that political analysis was colonizing the pulpit, mistaking strategy for gospel; others worried that adopting social-scientific tools imported worldviews hostile to faith; still others warned that zeal for justice could excuse cruelty to opponents. The movement answered in two ways. First, it emphasized method: tools are judged by whether they serve love of neighbor, especially the least protected. Second, it insisted on sacrament and prayer as guardrails: a people who confess sin together and submit to shared bread are less likely to turn opponents into prey. The goal was neither purity nor power as ends in themselves, but fidelity that could be audited by the poor.

Womanist insistence

Black women named omissions and set a new standard. They called out readings that treated "the poor" as if gender and family burdens did not exist; they confronted pulpits that celebrated male courage while women did logistics and childcare; they refused to let the story of oppression flatten differences within communities. Their theology drew on mothers' boards, kitchens, nurse's stations, schoolrooms, and storefronts—spaces where survival had long been managed—arguing that these were sites of revelation, not footnotes. Their exegesis lifted Hagar and Tamar, Mary and the women at the tomb; their ethics insisted that care work and wage work both be visible and valued. Congregational practice shifted: more women in visible leadership; budgets explicit about childcare; sermons careful to avoid romanticizing suffering kept on women's backs.

Seminaries and syllabi

Schools changed reading lists and assignments. Students read scripture with commentaries from the barrios, the rural South, the townships, and women's kitchens; they paired patristic texts with public-health histories; they set Augustine's City of God beside housing covenants and school zoning maps. Field education asked interns to keep two journals: one devotional, one observational—what did a neighborhood need, who already did the work, what could a church add or fix without paternalism? Evaluation rewarded accuracy and humility: a plan that built on existing networks counted more than a clever novelty. Faculty meetings learned new tensions: how to conserve the breadth of tradition while centering voices long excluded.

Ethics: from intent to impact

The moral test moved from motive to effect. Charity without structural repair was called what it was: relief that left injury unaddressed. Programs were measured by outcomes: did evictions decline, did graduation rates rise, did arrests for minor infractions shrink, did hospital admissions for preventable conditions fall? Sermons instructed congregations on the difference between optics and change: a well-attended rally versus a budget line moved; a viral photo versus a lease rewritten. The standard sharpened pastoral conscience and lay participation alike.[75]

Pastoral care in hard neighborhoods

Ministry in cities marked by disinvestment and surveillance demanded new craft. Clergy learned to triage requests without losing compassion, to build referral networks that did not trap people in humiliation, to sit with trauma that arrived layered—historic, daily, and anticipated. They trained lay visitors to recognize signs of depression and danger, to partner with social workers without surrendering agency, and to practice confidentiality in an era of theft and rumor. The care plan—so often invisible—was written down, held by teams, and revised when reality contradicted intention.

Global links and local lessons

International conversations fed local practice. Reports from Latin America's base communities, South Africa's church-sustained resistance, and Asian and African experiments with contextual theology returned with ideas: micro-credit tied to congregational accountability; literacy circles that doubled as rights education; clinics that trained community health workers; legal aid embedded in catechesis. The traffic ran both directions: strategies tested in American cities—tenant unions, police-community review, after-school ladders—were adapted abroad. What bound these exchanges was not uniform policy but shared method: begin with the most burdened; measure by what lifts them.[76]

Controversies, costs, and courage

To say "liberation" in some pulpits was to risk donor fatigue, denominational scrutiny, or political retaliation. Some pastors were removed; some congregations split; some projects lost city permits. The cost did not become a badge of honor; it became a line in a ledger that also recorded gains: a school integrated, a clinic opened, a policy revised, a youth diverted from prison into college. Leaders learned to celebrate quietly when quiet protected fragile advances and to speak loudly when silence was complicity. The courage required was rarely cinematic; it was procedural grit over years.

Budgets, audits, and trust

Trust remained the engine. Annual reports listed receipts and disbursements for clinics, schools, legal aid, and relief; independent audits underwrote grant requests and donor confidence; councils set caps on administrative overhead and stuck to them. Failures were acknowledged; course corrections were made in public; leaders rotated to prevent burnout and gatekeeping. A theology that preached truth about power practiced truth about its own numbers.

Youth and the next bench

The teenagers who carried signs in the 1960s grew into teachers, nurses, pastors, lawyers, and council members by the 1980s. Their apprentices were children who watched slide projectors and then VCRs play civil-rights footage on church walls, who read liberation primers in youth group, who visited shelters and clinics as field trips, and who learned that a good meeting needs an agenda and an end time. They wrote skits about fairness, argued in debates about policing and schools, sang songs that blended old spirituals with new harmonies, and took the offering with pride. Formation meant continuity: the next bench was never empty.

Media, message, and moral imagination

As television matured and local papers struggled, churches invested in media literacy. Press releases learned clarity without jargon; spokespersons trained to answer hostile questions without losing temper or tone; camera angles were chosen to preserve dignity and avoid exploitation. The message framed policy as neighbor love and prudence: good schools prevent crime; clinics save budgets; fair housing stabilizes blocks; jobs strengthen families. The imagination was moral and practical at once: a city worth living in is a theological claim and a municipal plan.

Liturgy of public life

Public ritual extended sanctuary claims into streets and chambers. Prayer vigils at hospitals protested closures; processions to city hall delivered petitions; blessing services commissioned teachers, janitors, bus drivers, and nurses for vocations honored as sacred. Church calendars incorporated school board meetings and budget hearings as congregational events; potlucks followed late-night votes; sanctuary announcements included legislative timelines. The city learned that this people would show up, stay late, and return with friends.

Failures named, lessons kept

Not every initiative endured. Clinics lost funding when political winds shifted; schools closed under pressures they could not overcome; partnerships frayed. The practice that kept the house together was frank accounting: what worked, what did not, what unintended harm had been done, what repair was owed. That honesty preserved credibility and taught younger leaders not to sanctify tactics that had outlived their usefulness. Theology kept pace: repentance for institutional harm sat beside laments for unjust losses.

Prayer, patience, and the long arc

The cadence of daily prayer kept the arc from breaking. Morning intercessions named tough meetings; evening thanksgivings counted small wins; weekly fasts sharpened attention; sabbaths reset bodies ground down by administration and advocacy. In sermons and in silences, leaders returned to durable texts: psalms that carried grief honestly, wisdom literature that trained prudence, prophetic oracles that refused to accept the status quo as natural. The long arc was not an excuse to be slow; it was a promise that allowed people to be steady.

By 1990, the vocabulary of liberation—preferential option for the poor, structural sin, contextual reading, base communities, womanist critique—had traveled from seminaries into bulletins and budgets. Congregations carried the habits forward into an era of megachurch growth, prosperity preaching, new immigration, and debates over gender and sexuality that would test both courage and charity. The next chapter tracks those tests: how institutions built by struggle navigated scale, money, media, generational change, and a widening Black Christian diaspora—holding fast to a God who sides with the burdened while learning new ways those burdens are carried.

Chapter 15

Faith in the 21st Century

A wider map, a faster clock

Since 1980, the ground beneath congregations has moved quickly: deindustrialization and suburbanization reshaped neighborhoods; cable, then internet, then social media reset attention; immigration remapped pews; higher education expanded expectations; disaffiliation rose; and public life polarized. Churches that once organized a ward now toggled between a sanctuary, a podcast, and a comment thread; that once printed bulletins now managed livestreams and text-to-give; that once sent a deacon to a city desk now tagged a councilmember on a platform and hosted a Zoom forum by nightfall. The habits built over a century—minutes, ledgers, choirs, clinics, coalitions—remained the bones, but the body moved in new ways.

Megachurch scale and the new campus

Across metro regions, some congregations grew to thousands, adding campuses, parking crews, security teams, broadcast studios, and staff lists that resembled small nonprofits. The Sunday schedule turned into a grid; the lobby into a concourse; the sanctuary into a set with cameras and light cues. Scale brought economies—clinics, scholarships, food banks, legal aid nights, job fairs—and vulnerabilities—overreliance on personality, brand over neighborhood, and the risk of anonymity within abundance. Governance stretched: boards learned risk management; finance teams mastered audits sized to seven figures; volunteer pipelines required training that looked like professional development. A megachurch could move pallets and policy; it could also miss a neighbor in need who slipped in and out unnoticed.[77]

Concrete examples make these dynamics palpable. Dallas's Potter's House, led by T. D. Jakes, long claims weekend attendance in the tens of thousands (commonly cited figures exceed 30,000 across multiple campuses and media audiences). Atlanta's New Birth Missionary Baptist Church under Eddie Long expanded to a multi-site ministry that membership tallies placed near 25,000 at its peak. Creflo Dollar's World Changers Church International similarly developed into a mass congregation with extensive media outreach and international ministries. These are not merely large worshiping bodies; they are institutional actors whose budgets, real estate holdings, and staffing structures resemble those of midsize nonprofits or small school districts.

That institutionalization is part of a broader statistical pattern. Since the late twentieth century, predominantly Black congregations were disproportionately represented among the fastest-growing congregations. In the 1970s and early 1980s there were only a handful of Black congregations consistently drawing weekend attendances above 2,000; by the 1990s and into the 2000s scores of predominantly Black congregations had reached megachurch scale. Nationwide counts of U.S. megachurches (commonly defined as churches averaging 2,000 or more in weekly attendance) rose from the low hundreds in the 1980s to well over a thousand by the early twenty-first century, and although the majority of these institutions were white-led, a visible and influential subset of them were Black-led and disproportionately visible in southern and urban metros. The rapid numerical growth reshaped denominational and civic religious landscapes,

placing Black megachurches squarely in conversations about political mobilization, social welfare provision, and media representation.

That reshaping is visible in programming as much as in pew counts.
Large Black congregations developed comprehensive social-service port-
folios that moved well beyond Sunday worship: on-site job training centers and workforce development partnerships with local employers; credit counseling services and congregational loan or credit-union experiments aimed at financial literacy and asset building; charter schools, after-school programs, and college-preparatory academies; regular free clinics and health screening events in partnership with hospitals; legal-aid
nights and tenant counseling; housing initiatives and community development corporations that pursue affordable housing projects. Potter's
House, for example, has become known not only for its televised worship
but for an array of community outreach programs—career fairs, scholarship funds, and food distribution—and Creflo Dollar's and New Birth's
ministries have likewise sponsored education and outreach events that blur
the line between parish ministry and community service provider. These
programs often fill gaps left by under resourced municipal services, giving
megachurches a civic as well as a spiritual profile.

But the financial and organizational scale that makes such programming
possible also complicates traditional modes of ecclesial oversight. Governance evolved from a parish-level model—where elders, deacons, and long-
standing lay leaders exercised day-to-day authority—to corporate forms
that require boards of directors, executive pastors, human-resources departments, and professional accountants. Boards learned to think in terms
of risk management, compliance, and public relations; finance teams developed internal controls and prepared for full external audits; legal counsel became a standing necessity as property holdings, payroll, and grant
management multiplied. Succession planning entered popular parish conversation in ways unfamiliar to older generations: who would follow a
charismatic founder? How does a board balance theological fidelity, pas-

toral charisma, and fiduciary responsibility? These questions are practical and existential. Where charismatic leadership accelerated growth, it also created concentrated authority that, when mishandled, generated crises. The 2010 sexual-misconduct allegations against Eddie Long and highly publicized stewardship controversies surrounding high-profile leaders such as Creflo Dollar (notably the debate over private-air travel and donor solicitation) made transparency, accountability, and outside oversight urgent institutional concerns. By contrast, leaders like T. D. Jakes—who invested in diversified programming, national media platforms, and a cadre of institutional leaders—offer a different model of founder influence and organizational entrenchment that some boards have been able to mediate more effectively.

The professionalization of staffing and volunteer management has subtle but profound effects on the internal culture of Black churches. Where a mid-century Black congregation might have been sustained by a rotating cast of unpaid lay ministers, choirs, and neighborhood stewards, a modern megachurch often employs full-time directors of community development, grant writers, campus pastors, and marketing teams. Lay engagement shifts from informal neighborly care to structured volunteer tracks with manuals, background checks, and performance evaluations. This produces efficiencies and widens the scope of ministry, but it also alters vocational patterns and modes of lay authority: elders who once exercised autonomous pastoral care now operate inside job descriptions and reporting lines.

These institutional shifts intersect uneasily with longstanding Black church traditions. Megachurches fulfill deep, historically rooted needs: they provide a place of spiritual uplift, a platform for Black leadership to gain public voice, and resources for social mobility and communal uplift. Large Sunday gatherings reproduce the Black pulpit's prophetic capacity to interpret suffering and hope on a mass scale; their economic initiatives continue the Black church's legacy as an incubator of self-help and mutual aid. At the same time, the megachurch model can challenge traditions of neighborhood solidarity, collective accountability, and grassroots activism. Consumerist dynamics—driven by branded preaching, stagecraft, and media markets—can prioritize attraction and retention over prophetic critique. The professionalization of ministry shifts power toward salaried staff and celebrity pastors, sometimes at the expense of the small-group, home-church, and mutual aid networks that historically sustained urban and rural Black communities. Moreover, the emphasis on growth metrics and campus expansion can reorient pastoral priorities toward institutional survival and brand management rather than the intensive, persistent presence in the lives of a geographically defined flock.

Thus the megachurch is a paradoxical heir to Black ecclesial history: it amplifies the church's capacity for social provision, civic presence, and spiritual formation while simultaneously renewing old tensions—between charismatic authority and congregational accountability, between institutional scale and neighborly intimacy, between market logics and prophetic ministry. For scholars and practitioners alike, the task is both analytical and prescriptive: to recognize the tangible benefits megachurches bring to Black communities—jobs, services, advocacy, and visibility—while pressing those same institutions to adopt governance practices, theological commitments, and community partnerships that guard against anonymity, fragmentation, and moral complacency.

Denominational contours and variations

- African Methodist Episcopal (AME) family. The AME and AME Zion traditions operate within an episcopal frame in which bishops and general conferences set doctrinal norms. Historically these bodies have issued statements upholding traditional sexual ethics, reflecting a theology of marriage as heterosexual and a pastoral conservatism rooted in communal stability and respectabil-

ity politics. Yet local AME congregations and some regional conferences have adopted more pastoral, less punitive approaches:
offering pastoral care without formal censure, quietly retaining
LGBTQ members in ministry roles, or sponsoring dialogues that
foreground pastoral well-being and the legacy of liberation theology. The result is institutional ambivalence—official reserve combined with local variety.

- Baptist traditions. Black Baptist life is not monolithic. National Baptist bodies (e.g., National Baptist Convention, USA) and
historic missionary conventions have tended toward conservative
positions on same-sex marriage and clergy discipline. Yet because
many Baptist congregations are congregationally governed, local
churches exhibit striking heterogeneity: some traditional downtown Black Baptist churches remain exclusionary; other congregations, often in college towns or urban contexts with younger
membership, have become intentionally affirming or have established formal non-discrimination policies. This congregational
polity produces rapid local change in some places and durable
conservatism in others.

- Pentecostal and Holiness sectors. Classic Pentecostal denominations with strong Black constituencies—most prominently the
Church of God in Christ (COGIC)—have generally maintained
explicit prohibitions against same-sex sexual expression in their
discipline manuals and pastoral teachings. The Pentecostal emphasis on holiness, bodily comportment, and charismatic authority has often made official change slow. Nonetheless, the charismatic impulse also produces grassroots experimentation: independent Black Pentecostal pastors, house churches, and neo-Pen-
tecostal congregations sometimes prioritize charismatic gifts and

pastoral outreach over juridical enforcement, resulting in local congregations where LGBTQ persons live and pray without formal recognition but with degrees of practical acceptance.

Theological debates within Black liberation and womanist frames

The dispute over sexuality and gender in Black churches cannot be reduced to social conservatism versus liberalism; it is, at root, a theological contest over the shape of liberation. James H. Cone's Black liberation theology supplies resources for rethinking sexual ethics: if theological reflection begins with the experience of the oppressed, then exclusion of marginalized sexual minorities is morally suspect because it betrays the theological priority of solidarity with the suffering. Womanist theologians—Jacquelyn Grant, Katie G. Cannon, Emilie Townes, and others—have further complicated the frame by insisting that gendered experience, sexual embodiment, and the survival strategies of Black women must inform ethical deliberation. These scholars critique heteronormativity as an instrument that can replicate domination within Black communities just as much as outside them.

At the same time, other influential Black theologians and pastors deploy scriptural literalism, pastoral prudence, and communal memory to defend traditional sexual ethics. For them, protecting the family as historically articulated is a pastoral strategy for communal flourishing in a racially hostile society. The theological argument therefore bifurcates along hermeneutical lines: one wing advances contextual, liberationist readings that place scripture's concern for the marginalized over literalist prohibitions; another insists on a moral coherence rooted in read-as-normative texts and pastoral concern for what they see as long-term communal stability. These positions are not merely intellectual; they signal different ecclesial imaginations about what it means for the church to be a refuge, a school of discipleship, and an agent of public witness.

Generational dynamics and leadership responses

Surveys and qualitative studies consistently show generational divergence. Younger Black Christians—particularly Millennials and members of Generation Z—are more likely to endorse same-sex marriage, to know openly LGBTQ persons, and to prioritize inclusion as a marker of Christian witness. Older generations often emphasize doctrinal fidelity, moral pedagogy, and social respectability. Pastors and denominational leaders therefore face a double bind: convert the younger constituency and risk alienating older, often financially central members; maintain older commitments and watch younger parishioners depart for more inclusive communities or disengage from church life entirely. Leadership responses reflect this tension. Some senior pastors and bishops have doubled down on disciplinary measures and public pronouncements reaffirming traditional teaching; others have adopted a pastoralist stance—emphasizing welcome, covenantal love, and a reluctance to prescribe sexual ethics publicly while continuing private pastoral counsel. A third group of leaders has attempted mediated positions: instituting anti-harassment policies, opening formal conversation series, or creating structured spaces for deliberation that seek to hold together doctrinal boundaries and relational hospitality.

This set of leadership choices is shaped in large part by a demographic and cultural reality often summarized as "belonging before believing." The phrase captures a recurrent pattern among millennials and Gen Z: membership in or attachment to a congregation is more frequently motivated by relational, cultural, and affective ties than by assent to a fixed set of doctrinal propositions. Empirically, this shift is visible in broader participation and affiliation trends. Surveys from major research organizations place the religiously unaffiliated proportion of young adults in the United States in a substantially larger range than earlier cohorts; Pew Research Center's Religious Landscape data first identified roughly a third of 18–29-year-olds as religiously unaffiliated (about 35–36 percent) and more recent studies by Pew, PRRI, and Barna document continued growth in unaffiliated identity among younger cohorts, with variation by question wording, geography, and race (see Pew Research Center; PRRI; Barna Group). Likewise, measures of weekly worship attendance have declined across generational cohorts over the past two decades (Gallup and other trackers report a steady fall in reported weekly attendance from the late 1990s into the 2010s and 2020s), and research on voluntary associations shows that young adults are more likely than previous generations to participate episodically rather than commit to formal membership rolls (Smith, 2011; Wuthnow, 2019).

Within Black American Christianity the numbers mask complexity: Black young adults are less likely than white peers to be unaffiliated overall, and many continue to identify cultural and communal ties to historically Black churches even when their patterns of participation change (Cose & McRoberts; Pew analyses of race and religion). But the ways in which Black congregations cultivate belonging are changing—and these changes are precisely what leaders are responding to when they recalibrate pastoral priorities, redesign ministry programs, and reimagine institutional boundaries. Looking forward, that recalibration must reckon with three concrete structural forces—artificial intelligence, climate change, and demographic transformation—that will reshape ministry contexts, organizational capacity, and theological priorities over the next decades.[78]

1. How AI, climate change, and demographic shifts will impact Black churches

- Artificial intelligence. In the coming decade AI will touch nearly every administrative and ministerial function of congregational life. Routine tasks—membership databases, scheduling, donation processing, neighborhood outreach lists—will be increasingly automated, lowering transaction costs for small congregations if they can access and steward the tools. Sermon preparation, biblical research, and pastoral counseling may also be augmented by AI-generated drafts, summaries of theological literature, and conversation aids. At the same time AI poses theological and ethical questions: who authors the message of the church when algorithmic inputs shape preaching; what safeguards protect pastoral confidentiality when third-party platforms mediate counseling; how do bias and surveillance embedded in AI systems affect congregants of color? If access to high-quality AI tools and training is uneven, existing resource disparities among Black congregations may widen, privileging well-resourced megachurches and networks while smaller, poorer parishes fall further behind.[79]

- Climate change. Climatic volatility—more frequent heat waves, floods, storms, and displacement—will disproportionately affect Black communities already vulnerable because of historical segregation, housing inequality, and environmental racism. Black churches will increasingly be called to serve as emergency hubs: shelters, distribution centers, healing spaces, and coordination points for recovery. They will also be asked to take prophetic and practical stances on ecological justice—advocating for policies that reduce exposure to pollution, investing in resilience measures (cooling centers, solar backup systems, flood mitigation for campus properties), and integrating ecological care into liturgy and discipleship. The fiscal and organizational demands of such roles require both new capacities and external partnerships.

- Demographic shifts. Two demographic patterns deserve emphasis. First, aging of long-time congregants coupled with episodic participation among younger cohorts creates a sustainability gap in volunteer labor, financial giving, and leadership succession. Second, the Black population in the United States is changing shape—through internal migration (urban revival, Southern growth), suburbanization, and continued immigration from Africa and the Caribbean—bringing linguistic, liturgical, and cultural pluralism into congregational life. These shifts yield both tensions (competing worship styles, generational expectations) and opportunities (new ministries, transnational partnerships, broader civic influence).

2. Emerging leadership models and technological adaptations

- Leaders who will thrive in this environment will not be simply those who replicate existing models more efficiently, but those who reconfigure authority, deployment of talent, and use of technology.

- Distributed leadership and networked ministry. Bi-vocational pastors, lay ecclesial ministers, and ministry teams that combine digital coordinators, social organizers, and liturgical artists will become more common. Clerical authority will be exercised alongside trained laity who can lead neighborhood response teams, manage online small groups, and curate digital worship experiences.[80]

- Hybrid and modular ministry. Worship and formation that intentionally mix in-person and virtual modalities—livestreamed preaching with localized small group practice, asynchronous discipleship curricula, mobile outreach backed by geospatial data—will become normative. Churches that develop robust digital discipleship ecosystems (with secure platforms for pastoral care) will engage younger cohorts more effectively.

- Tech-savvy pastoral formation. Seminaries and denominational training bodies must teach not merely tech skills, but tech literacy grounded in ethics: data stewardship, digital pastoral boundaries, AI literacy, and discernment frameworks for new media. Partnerships with Black theologians and ethicists are essential to shape culturally grounded digital practices.

3. Generational succession: challenges and opportunities

Succession will be one of the defining institutional questions of the next twenty years.

Challenges:

- Financial precarity and property costs may force congregations to shrink or repurpose campuses, making traditional full-time pastoral models less sustainable.

- Intergenerational dis-junctures over form and content of worship, polity, and public witness can create conflict at moments of transition.

- Young Black leaders often face the choice of secular careers or NGO work that offers more predictable income than parish ministry.

Opportunities:

- Apprenticeship models, shared pastoral circuits, and stipend residencies can create pathways for younger leaders without depending solely on single churches' budgets.

- Intentional intergenerational covenanting—structured mentoring, shared decision-making bodies, and joint social projects—can preserve institutional memory while enabling innovation.

- New vocational imaginaries (social entrepreneurship, civic chaplaincy, arts-based ministries) expand where and how pastoral gifts are exercised, keeping the church centrally involved in communal life even if institutional forms evolve.

4. Theological reflection on continuity and change

Theologically, the primary resource of the Black church is its capacity to hold together prophetic critique and embodied solidarity—public witness against injustice while forming loving, sacramental communities. Continuity must be sought not in static liturgical forms alone but in the underlying commitments that have sustained Black Christian witness: a theology of liberation that centers God's preferential concern for the poor and oppressed; a communal soteriology that sees salvation in social as well as personal dimensions; and an incarnational hermeneutic that reads scripture through the lived experience of Black life.

Change should therefore be assessed by whether innovations preserve those commitments. Tech adaptations that enhance pastoral care, ecological practices that embody stewardship and justice, and leadership reforms that broaden participation are theologically consonant when they deepen the church's capacity to love, to bind wounds, and to stand against structural sin. Conversely, any technological or organizational shift that undermines prophetic clarity, commodifies the gospel, or disintegrates communal accountability calls for theological resistance. This requires robust theological education for both clergy and laity that is rooted in Black interpretive traditions—preaching, music, and narrative theology—and engaged with contemporary ethical questions about technology and ecology.

5. Specific recommendations for church resilience and adaptation

- Leadership responses reflect this tension. Some senior pastors and bishops have doubled down on disciplinary measures and public pronouncements reaffirming traditional teaching; others have adopted a pastoralist stance—emphasizing welcome, covenantal love, and a reluctance to prescribe sexual ethics publicly while continuing private pastoral counsel. A third group of leaders has attempted mediated positions: instituting anti-harassment policies, opening formal conversation series, or creating structured spaces for deliberation that seek to hold together doctrinal boundaries and relational hospitality. Leaders may adopt pastoralist or mediated strategies.

These examples show practical patterns that recur where belonging precedes belief:

- Hospitality and low-barrier entry points. Newcomers are invited to meals, service projects, music nights, or discussion groups without formal membership interviews or doctrinal tests. The emphasis is on welcome and relationship building.

- Small relational cohorts. Covenant groups, mentorship pairs, and communal "pods" are promoted as primary loci of formation rather than large institutional classes. These groups provide mutual accountability and spiritual conversation in a context often framed by shared commitments to justice or vocation rather than creedal precision.

- Service and justice as catechesis. Participation in food banks, voter drives, housing clinics, or police-accountability campaigns functions as theological formation in practice; meaning and identity are cultivated through shared action.

- Hybrid digital-physical engagement. Churches deploy social me-

dia, livestreamed worship, and group messaging to sustain relationships outside Sunday worship, reflecting young adults' expectation of ongoing, digitally mediated community.

- Aesthetic and cultural resonance. Music, arts, and culturally
competent preaching that reflect young adults' lived realities are
prioritized to generate affective connection prior to doctrinal instruction.

How does this differ from traditional membership models? Traditional
models in many Black churches have emphasized formal affiliation—public confession of faith, baptism (where applicable), enrollment on membership rolls, regular attendance, and economic contribution—as markers of belonging. The pastoral authority model assumed that once one
was "in" the congregation, theological instruction, denominational identity, and institutional obligations followed. By contrast, the belonging-
first model decouples initial belonging from immediate doctrinal con-
formity or full institutional commitment. It privileges relational capital—friendship, mentorship, shared work—and treats doctrinal formation
as a process that may be gradual, voluntary, and oriented toward praxis.

This difference has several analytic implications:

- Mobility and fluidity. Young adults increasingly engage on a part-
time, project-based basis. Churches that assume durable attendance and immediate formal membership may miss opportunities
to steward nascent loyalties into deeper commitments.

- Authority and pedagogy. Where formal membership once carried clear expectations enforced by church leadership, belonging-
first contexts distribute authority more horizontally—through
peer leaders, program coordinators, and social networks—alter-
ing pastoral strategies for discipleship and discipline.

- Theological pluralism within communities. Congregations that prioritize belonging often tolerate a wider range of theological positions among participants. The risk and the possibility here are both ecclesial: risk insofar as core doctrinal boundaries may blur; possibility insofar as diverse convictions can be held within a covenantal habitat that bears collective witness.

Successful programming that exemplifies belonging-before-believing includes:

- Service projects with embedded formation: weekly food pantry shifts combined with short reflection sessions and mentoring that link practice with theological reflection (many urban Black churches use this model).

- Justice campaigns that invite sustained involvement: voter registration drives, prison rehabilitation partnerships, and police-accountability coalitions that mobilize young adults and integrate them into leadership teams.

- Reading groups and book clubs: facilitated discussions of contemporary theology, social ethics, and literature (e.g., reading Ta-Nehisi Coates alongside church histories) that provide intellectual pathways into faith conversations without immediate doctrinal tests.

- Vocational cohorts and entrepreneurship programs: opportunities for young adults to receive practical support (resume workshops, microloans) in community with pastoral care, which builds reciprocal loyalty and trust.

- Arts and worship labs: collaborative music or drama ensembles that contribute to worship leadership and create tangible roles for young adults.

The turn to belonging before believing is not an isolated ecclesial fad but a particular expression of broader generational shifts: greater institutional skepticism, a premium on authenticity and experience, heightened social-justice orientation, and digital-first habits. For Black young adults, racialized experiences and community expectations intersect with these trends in distinctive ways—many still value the Black church as a cultural and political home even as they demand different forms of participation and leadership.

For church leaders, the analytic task is not merely to choose between doctrinal firmness and pastoral openness but to design practices that can translate belonging into durable theological formation. That requires intentional pathways: low-barrier entry points that lead to covenantal small groups, service engagements that incorporate reflective theology, and leadership pipelines that confer responsibility and doctrinal teaching in relational contexts. Without such pathways, belonging risks remaining episodic. With them, belonging can become the soil in which belief, discipleship, and intergenerational continuity are cultivated.

Some congregations adopt discretionary pathways that allow LGBTQ members to participate in ministries and community life without conferring formal recognition or ordination. The varieties of response often correlate with ecclesial polity (episcopal leaders can enforce discipline at scale; congregational polity allows local experimentation), the demographic profile of the congregation, and the political ecology of the metropolitan area.

Congregational case studies: navigating inclusion debates

- The suburban megachurch case. In several Sun Belt cities, large predominantly Black megachurches have publicly wrestled with inclusion when a prominent staff person or music leader came out. In some cases, leadership opted for negotiated exits to avoid polarization; in others, public town-hall meetings produced fractious departures and the formation of small offshoot fellowships. These megachurches typically weigh reputation, philanthropic partnerships, and denominational ties in choosing a course.[81]

- The historic downtown congregation. A century-old downtown Baptist church with deep roots in the civil rights era faced a sustained debate after young adults organized a series of sermons and panel discussions on sexuality and justice. The result was a negotiated compromise: an official reaffirmation of historic teaching coupled with a new commitment to pastoral care ministries for LGBTQ persons and a youth-sponsored social justice initiative. The congregation retained most members but endured ongoing tension.

- Newer affirming congregations and networks. Where institutional doors remained closed, Black LGBTQ Christians and allies formed alternative ecclesial spaces—house churches, networks of affirming pastors, and ecumenical fellowships. Organizations such as the Fellowship of Affirming Ministries (FAM) and local affirming Black congregations intentionally blend Pentecostal worship styles and Black cultural idioms with explicit LGBTQ inclusion, creating sanctuaries that reconfigure traditional rhythms of Black church life.

Connection to civil-rights history and intersectional critique The Black church's central role in the civil-rights movement creates both resources and constraints. On the one hand, the movement established the Black church as a moral and political locus with claims on national conscience; this legacy supplies rhetorical capital for leaders who argue that the church should be at the forefront of expanding dignity. On the other hand, civil-rights organizing historically prioritized race and, in many institutional settings, deferred or sidelined questions of sexuality and gender to preserve political coalitions. The marginalization of openly queer civil-rights leaders—most notably Bayard Rustin—offers a cautionary tale of how strategic political considerations can reproduce intramural exclusions.

Intersectionality reframes the debate by insisting that race, gender, class, and sexuality are mutually constitutive. For Black LGBTQ persons, exclusion from Black churches compounds societal marginalization. An intersectional theological ethics emphasizes that commitments to racial justice require attention to all axes of oppression. Theological formation that ignores intersectionality risks perpetuating forms of respectability politics that police bodies and identities in the name of communal advancement.

Institutional consequences: membership change, schism, and realignment Decisions about sexuality and gender identity have measurable institutional consequences. Congregations that move toward official inclusion often experience short-term tension and, in some cases, the departure of older or more conservative members. Conversely, exclusionary or punitive stances can precipitate the loss of younger members, professionals, and families who prioritize inclusive belonging. Some denominations experience institutional schisms: local churches withdrawing, new associations forming, and clergy moving between networks. Yet these outcomes are uneven and mediated by local leadership, financial resilience, and community context.

A further institutional consequence is the reconfiguration of space: as some traditional Black churches double down on conservative teaching, new spaces—affirming Black congregations, queer-centered ministries, and interfaith networks—emerge to absorb religious energy that traditional institutions will not contain. These dynamic shifts reveal that containment strategies—whether disciplinary or pastoralist—are not decisive; they are part of a longer trajectory of institutional adaptation.

Concluding synthesis: theological practice and accountable leadership

The tensions are not merely administrative; they are theological and pastoral. Making progress requires denominational and congregational leaders who can translate theological conviction into accountable governance—policies that protect vulnerable members, transparent processes for dispute, and sustained theological education that engages scripture, tradition, and the lived realities of congregants. For Black churches committed to social justice, the integrity of their witness will increasingly be measured by how they hold the multiply marginalized—not by how well they preserve institutional comfort.

The challenge, then, is to cultivate theological resources that honor both the prophetic memory of the Black freedom struggle and the bodily claims of LGBTQ persons whose lives intersect with that memory. Practically this looks like: episcopal bodies using their authority to convene rigorous theological inquiry rather than merely issuing bans; congregational pastors fostering disciplined, theologically informed conversation rather than reactive denunciation; and denominational networks creating pathways for accountability that do not default to anonymity or ostracism. Only by attending both to theological truth and pastoral justice can Black churches navigate these debates without repeating old patterns of exclusion under a new set of institutional pressures.

This pattern often resulted in the misuse of authority and the marginalization of the very neighborhoods that spawned them: as institutional power concentrated around charismatic leadership and centralized budgets, decision-making moved away from local participation, resources were allocated toward programmatic visibility and campus expansion rather than neighborhood needs, and long-standing networks of mutual aid and grassroots accountability were sidelined—outcomes that left nearby residents less served, less consulted, and less able to hold their own churches to the communal responsibilities those institutions once embodied.[82]

Prosperity currents and their counterpoint

The prosperity gospel—preaching health and wealth as covenant benefits—rose in visibility through televangelism and, later, streaming. For some, it offered hope of reversal and a grammar of gratitude in communities long denied credit, care, and capital; for critics, it risked sanctifying market logic, blaming the poor for systemic injuries, and centering leaders' lifestyles. The counterpoint held to older social-gospel and liberation instincts: preach generosity without promising return, name structures without resigning personal agency, and invest offerings into schools, clinics, mutual aid, and legal help. The pastoral craft was to teach contentment without training passivity, ambition without baptizing greed, and testimony without turning God into a vending machine.

On a bright Sunday in suburban Atlanta you can feel the difference before you step inside. At World Changers Church International, the cameras are rolling. The stage is a blaze of light, the choir answers with tightly choreographed praise, and a young woman steps to the mic to testify that after sowing a "seed" she landed a job, bought a used car, and finally saw her credit repaired. The sermon that morning — Creflo Dollar's signature mix of scripture and fiscal promise — names prosperity as a covenant right: God's will, the preacher says, is for families to move from scarcity into visible blessing. The language is electric, intimate, and measurable: healings, promotions, houses, children in new schools. For many in the pews, these sermons are tonic — a theology that reframes dignity as tangible return, a grammar of gratitude for people who have long been denied credit, care, and capital.

Across the city, in a century-old brownstone that houses the Abyssinian Baptist Church's outreach programs, the rhythm is different. The sermon there — following a history of Adam Clayton Powell and, more recently, the social investments of Calvin O. Butts III — slides from scripture into the particulars of Harlem life: the precariousness of subway jobs, a mother's eviction notice, the neighborhood clinic's dwindling funds. After worship, volunteers fold boxes of fresh produce, lawyers from a clinic take calls in a liturgy of logistics, and a young man signs up for a GED class that the church underwrites. Few promises are made about immediate wealth; instead the pulpit insists on structural naming and patient, collective work. The emphasis is clear: generosity without guaranteeing a return, and investment in schools, clinics, and mutual aid rather than in a personal windfall.

These are not two neat tribes but overlapping convictions and constant conversations. T.D. Jakes's Potter's House, for example, blends covenantal assurance with community programs that feed families and coach entrepreneurs. The tension shows on ordinary faces: a single mother who wonders whether to give her last $20 as a "seed" and pray for a miracle, or to use it to pay the bus fare to a job interview she secured through a church staffing referral. A retired teacher, grateful for a parking-lot testimony of a recovered health insurance claim, quietly asks whether such messages sometimes make poverty a moral failing rather than a policy problem.

Scholars and critics — from historians of the Word of Faith movement to writers like Kate Bowler — point out the risks: sanctifying market logic, centering pastoral lifestyles, or blaming those crushed by systemic injustice. The pastoral craft, then, becomes a kind of moral tightrope: teaching contentment without training passivity, encouraging ambition without baptizing greed, celebrating testimony without turning God into a vending machine. In the end, the most persuasive sermons are those that refuse the false choice: they hold open both promise and responsibility, personal uplift and communal repair — and, in doing so, keep faith oriented toward both salvation and solidarity.

Digital church: from microphone to camera

The pivot to digital began with radio, expanded with cable, then democratized with platforms that put broadcast within reach of any phone. Pastors learned to write for two rooms at once—the people in the pews and the lens beyond the back wall. Musicians mixed for earbuds and subwoofers; ushers became chat moderators; greeters moved to comment threads. During public emergencies, digital held congregations together: prayer chains turned into video rooms; small groups met across time zones; funerals blended in-person and remote participation. Digital reach multiplied audiences and offerings; it also demanded ethics: data privacy, consent for images, avoiding spectacle over substance, and guarding against algorithmic drift toward outrage.

When COVID-19 slammed doors shut, many Black churches found themselves improvising a sacred technology overnight. One Saturday night a pastor whose best skill had been extemporaneous preaching sat in his living room with a borrowed tripod, a neighbor's ring light, and a pile of hymnals. He learned to frame a sermon for a phone camera, to modulate his voice for a microphone that picked up the hum of the fridge. Within days his small staff had become producers: teenagers learned OBS and audio mixing on YouTube tutorials; a choir director began teaching harmony over grainy Zoom audio; an elder with a landline figured out how to bridge phone callers into the livestream so those without smartphones could still "attend."[83]

Those improvisations produced tender, human moments that no polished production could replicate. A widow at home who had not left the house in months waved at the camera and mouthed the Lord's Prayer; family members abroad tuned in and left comments that read like prayers.

After a much-loved matriarch's funeral, the church livestream drew siblings who had not spoken in years — they watched, grieved, and reconciled together in a way that physical distance had not allowed. A youth ministry that had been padding weekly attendance with pizza and games shifted to asynchronous Bible studies on WhatsApp, where teens shared scripture screenshots, voice notes, and short testimonies between homework assignments.

The pivot was also full of practical headaches. Internet bandwidth and cell coverage varied by neighborhood; mid-sermon freeze frames became part of the liturgy. Volunteers learned to compress video, set up hotspot backups, and schedule pre-recorded segments to cover outages. Zoom-bombing early on forced password-protected rooms and waiting rooms — an unwelcome lesson in online security. Churches scrambled to add online giving, navigating payment processors, transaction fees, and the confusion of first-time users. Many had to decide whether to pay for captioning services or rely on imperfect automated captions, an accessibility choice with both moral and budgetary consequences.

Ethics moved from abstract policy to everyday decisions. Leaders wrestled with consent for posting images — a baptism image shared for outreach could unintentionally expose a child. Pastors resisted the temptation to chase clicks with provocative sermon titles, reminding one another that the faith they preached couldn't be reduced to viral spectacle. They also confronted algorithmic drift: what the platform rewarded (outrage, short clips, hot takes) did not always reward pastoral care and theological nuance. So churches developed guidelines: clear consent forms for recording, careful stewardship of contact lists, and a commitment to publish full sermons alongside highlight reels to preserve substance.

Out of strain came invention. Virtual choirs were assembled from dozens of individual recordings stitched into one hymn; drive-in services offered communion packets and live-streamed prayer; phone trees and "wellness teams" made rounds that digital platforms could not. The digital church multiplied reach, but it also revealed what mattered most — the call to belong, to listen, and to protect one another in a new terrain where ministry and morality met bandwidth and code.

Disaffiliation and resilient cores

The rise of the religiously unaffiliated reshaped the landscape, especially among younger adults. Yet within Black church traditions, resilient cores persisted: choir-centered worship, strong pastoral identity, rituals of care, and a culture of belonging that carried families through births, graduations, layoffs, and grief. Congregations responded to disaffiliation with mixed strategies—apologetics series for skeptics; service projects that opened faith through action; arts programs that invited participation without pressure; and honest forums for doubt that refused to punish questions. The wager was simple: lived credibility and communal warmth could outrun caricature; integrity could outlast trend lines.

Global Black Christianity at home

Immigration from Africa and the Caribbean brought new languages, rhythms, expectations, and ecclesial models. Nigerian, Ghanaian, Ethiopian-Eritrean, Congolese, Haitian, Jamaican, and Trinidadian congregations planted storefronts and then purchased warehouses; prayer styles intensified—night vigils, fasting calendars, deliverance ministries; networks spanned WhatsApp groups that tied Atlanta to Accra, London, and Lagos in a weeknight prayer chain. Cross-pollination followed: African diasporic churches adopted local social-service models; historically Black American congregations borrowed all-night prayer and deliverance language; joint services lined up steelpan with Hammond organ, highlife with hymnody. The shared grammar was urgency, reverence, and family.[84]

On a late-summer Sunday in a Brooklyn storefront sanctuary, the service begins with the slow, familiar lift of a Baptist hymn — organ swelling, voices rising in four-part harmony — and then, without a seam, a lead singer in a bright Ankara dress launches into a Nigerian praise chorus. The congregation answers: some with the measured, seated sway they learned in Black Baptist pews; others with the high, syncopated clapping and ululating responses of West African Pentecostalism. Drums that would have been polite accessories in a mid-century AME service now puncture the hymn's cadence, and the soloist alternates between the shape-note runs of an old spiritual and ornamented Yoruba phrases. This is not a collision but a conversation, an audible map of migration and memory.

Across town in Flatbush, Brooklyn, Haitian Creole prayers curl around an AME liturgy. After the sermon, an elder woman rises, voice coarse with years of outdoor market calling and hard work; she prays in Creole, invoking saints and ancestors in a cadence that matches the call-and-response the AME choir has been practicing all month. Choir members instinctively echo back in English, translating and harmonizing on the fly. The result is a bilingual, kinesthetic prayer where the rhythms of both traditions bend to make room for one another: hearty "amens" punctuate "Mèsi, Senyè" (Thank you, Lord), and the pastor — trained in the historical rhythms of Black Methodist preaching — pauses to receive a benediction passed in Creole.

These scenes have institutional anchors. Large diasporic churches such as Redeemed Christian Church of God (RCCG) parishes in Atlanta and Houston routinely share worship styles with neighborhood Baptist and AME congregations, while landmark Black churches like Abyssinian Baptist Church in Harlem host visiting choirs and choirs-in-residence from the Caribbean and Africa. Neighborhoods — Little Haiti in Miami, East Flatbush and Crown Heights in Brooklyn, Dorchester and Mattapan in Boston, Bronzeville in Chicago — become nodes where music, liturgy, and pastoral practice are traded, tested, and transformed.

Technology amplifies the blend. WhatsApp prayer chains bind diasporic families across oceans: a Lagos pastor posts a five-minute exhortation; a second-generation congregant in Brooklyn forwards it at dawn with a voice note: "Play this at prayer tonight." By evening, the church's WhatsApp group is a tapestry of voice clips, emoji candles, and requests for intercession, and the sermon references sermons heard in Accra and Port-au-Prince. Live-streamed services from Lagos or Port-au-Prince are watched on phones in the back pew while children color; hymns are learned via YouTube clips; choir repertoires now routinely include anthems with creole refrains, Yoruba call-and-response sections, and agreeably stretched southern gospel harmonies.

These cross-pollinations are tactile and sensory: the scent of coconut oil on a Sunday hat at a Caribbean-inflected baptism, the metallic snap of tambourine against hymnals, a pastor switching languages mid-sermon because the week's new immigrant family only understands one. The result is a contemporary Black Christianity that is insistently local and thoroughly global — a practiced bricolage in which faith is not simply imported or inherited but remade in song, prayer, and hospitality.

Music's great remix

Worship expanded along several lines at once: traditional choir and pipe organ; contemporary gospel with full rhythm sections; praise-and-worship imports from multiracial evangelical spaces revoiced through Black aesthetics; hip-hop and spoken word as proclamation; and hymnody revived through call-and-response. Choir robes met denim; robes returned for anniversaries; praise flags waved at one service while a string quartet played at another. The throughline remained participatory power: congregational singing as formation, teaching, and balm. Musicians became theologians by setlist; sound engineers became liturgists with faders; and licensing taught the legal side of the new sound.

Women at the center—again, and more visibly

Women who long held calendars and checkbooks increasingly held pulpits and presidencies: senior pastors, bishops in Pentecostal and Holiness streams, seminary deans, denominational officers, lead chaplains, heads of faith-based nonprofits. Their leadership altered tone and attention: maternal health clinics, domestic-violence shelters, girls' mentorship scaled; pastoral care systems professionalized; budget lines for childcare and counseling normalized. Resistance persisted in some quarters; the response was steady performance, rigorous preparation, thick networks, and an unapologetic theological case for gifts recognized at last.

By the late twentieth century the pattern shifted from quiet exception to visible leadership because generations of women had learned how to perform competence so consistently that it became impossible to dismiss. The story is not abstract; it is full of faces, fights, and midnight phone calls.

Consider Jarena Lee's long-ago insistence on preaching in the early nineteenth century — she bargained for a chance and then kept returning until Black Methodist leaders could not ignore her gifts. Fast forward to the modern era and the stakes are higher but the method is the same: show up, do the work, outlast the objections. Leontine T. C. Kelly, elected a bishop in the United Methodist Church in 1984, became a model of steady performance: sermon after sermon, program after program, the calm pastoral competence that made critics' objections look petty beside congregations that were thriving under her leadership. When Barbara Clementine Harris was consecrated in 1989 as the first woman bishop in the Anglican Communion (Episcopal Church), the spectacle included angry protests and doomsaying from conservative corners. What the headlines sometimes missed was the years of parish-level labor Harris had done — hospital visits, pastoral counseling, patient administration — that secured the trust of people who mattered most: parishioners whose lives were improved by her care.

Vashti Murphy McKenzie's election as the first female bishop of the African Methodist Episcopal Church in 2000 carried similar drama. Her campaign through annual conferences meant navigating political conventions long dominated by men; she had to prove her administrative acuity and theological seriousness in ways male candidates were rarely asked to demonstrate. The double standard was palpable: women were judged for a single misstep that men shrugged off. These women answered that calculus with what critics later called "thick networks": intentional mentorship circles that functioned like on-ramps. Yvette Flunder, founder of City of Refuge and the Fellowship of Affirming Ministries, turned her church in the Bay Area into a training ground for clergy who were marginalized elsewhere — women, LGBTQ leaders, and people living with HIV. Her fellowship offered ordination pathways, clergy support groups, and congregational training in inclusive theology.

The specific programs matter. Katie Geneva Cannon and other womanist theologians developed curricula and workshops that became models for seminaries and congregational education; clergy cohorts formed around those syllabi, sharing sermon critiques, job leads, and childcare plans so women could accept longer pastoral assignments. Practical mentorship looked like the retired pastor who wrote a glowing recommendation that opened a door, the dean who assigned a pulpit when a young preacher's resume needed sermons-in-hand, the informal phone tree that mobilized summer relief funds so a pastor could complete an advanced degree.

Human drama — the late-night sermon rewrites, the whispered committee conversations, the congregants who wept when a woman finally sat in the bishop's chair — makes the shift vivid. Through steady performance, rigorous preparation, thick networks, and an unapologetic theological defense of their call, these women did more than win positions. They changed the expectations of what Black Christian leadership could look like, and in the process taught an institutional religion how to recognize gifts it had too long taken for granted.

Public witness: from marches to policy briefs

The turn of the century saw churches reenter streets and chambers with new coalitions: criminal-justice reform campaigns, voting-rights protections, police oversight, lead-pipe replacement, school funding equalization, hospital closures contested, gun-violence interventions launched. The toolkit matured: Sunday sermons set the moral arc; weekday briefings presented data; "Souls to the Polls" revived old cadences; court-watch teams sat through arraignments; restorative-justice circles met in fellowship halls; trauma-informed pastors sat on task forces. The ethic remained pastoral: protect the vulnerable, tell the truth, do the work, give grace where possible, draw a line where necessary.

Trauma, counseling, and clinical partnership

Pastoral care increasingly included licensed counseling and referrals for depression, anxiety, grief, addiction, and family violence. Churches hosted clinicians; trained lay counselors; normalized therapy from the pulpit; and integrated mental-health checks into youth and men's ministries. After mass traumas—police shootings, pandemics, storms—sanctuaries became clinics for the soul and body: vaccine drives, grief groups, financial triage, tutoring to catch up missed school. The old line about "pray and push" became "pray and go to therapy," with the same urgency and less stigma.[85]

Money, transparency, and trust

Scandals in the broader religious ecosystem raised stakes for transparency. Budgets posted, audits published, conflict-of-interest policies written, whistleblower protections established, compensation bands disclosed, and capital campaigns professionalized. Digital giving made generosity easier and grift easier; controls tightened: dual approvals, outside reviews, donor-intent tracking, and sunset clauses. Trust—always the currency—became measurable: satisfaction surveys, retention data, and the simplest test—would the people call this place first in a storm?

Education: ladders still rising

Church-anchored schools, after-school programs, tutoring, and college-access pipelines scaled with new partners. FAFSA nights and SAT prep shared calendars with coding camps, makerspaces, and dual-enrollment counseling. Scholarship funds got smarter—mentorship tied to money; persistence checks each term; emergency micro-grants to prevent dropout over a $600 bill. The old pride in graduation Sundays grew new layers: first-gen ceremonies; trade-school blessings; licensing prayers for nurses and teachers; and job fairs hosted with unions and tech firms.

Policing, safety, and pastoral presence

Congregations learned the hard craft of safety without turning sanctuaries into fortresses. Safety teams trained in de-escalation and first aid; ushers learned to spot distress; pastors reviewed security footage and also wrote letters asking prosecutors for alternatives to incarceration. Police partnerships existed where possible; accountability coalitions formed where necessary. Funerals after violence remained terrible liturgies of truth; altar calls for peace were paired with enrollment for conflict-interruption programs.

LGBTQ+ debates and degrees of welcome

Questions of sexuality and gender identity pressed congregations and denominations into long, often painful discernment. Across the landscape, responses varied: full inclusion with weddings and ordinations; "welcoming but not affirming" postures; explicit exclusions; and many in-between realities shaped by pastoral relationships. Where debates stayed human—names, stories, shared prayer—bonds sometimes held; where debates abstracted into slogans, breaks hardened. Youth ministries navigated this tension up close, insisting on safety and dignity for all while leaders argued doctrine. The best practices were consistent: clarity without cruelty, policy before crisis, and an open door for conversation even after a vote.[86]

Black-led evangelical streams and their tensions

In multiracial evangelical spaces, Black pastors and worship leaders grew large platforms, bringing gospel idioms and justice themes into settings that alternately celebrated and resisted them. Conflicts surfaced around race, policing, immigration, and nationalism; departures followed when lines could not be reconciled. Out of those tensions, new networks formed—churches grounded in evangelical piety and Black social ethics, hybrid liturgies, and tactical independence from donor blocs allergic to structural critique. The cost was real; so was the freedom to preach without asterisks.

Entrepreneurship, bi-vocational ministry, and tents

Pastors worked with tents again—bi-vocational by design or necessity: teachers, counselors, contractors, coders, chaplains, non-profit directors. The model diversified income and strengthened credibility in the marketplace; it also stretched time and demanded disciplined sabbath. Entrepreneurial congregations launched co-working spaces, cafes, print shops, and arts venues in church buildings to anchor daytime presence on commercial corridors neglected by capital. The principle remained parish-based: make the block better between Sundays.

Arts, beauty, and belonging

Choirs remained, but so did liturgical dance, theater, mural projects, galleries, and film screenings. Beauty became argument: the neighborhood is worth color, craft, and care; the child is worth a violin; the hallway is worth framed photographs of elders with names and dates. Artists received residencies; commissions memorialized saints and struggles; spoken-word nights braided faith, doubt, and hope. In a noisy era, the church's aesthetic said, "Slow down; this matters."

Global links renewed

Diaspora ties matured past nostalgia into strategic partnership: scholarships from U.S. congregations funded seminary seats in Nairobi; Ghanaian churches sent prayer teams and small business mentors to U.S. plants; Haitian congregations trained American youth in disaster response on mission trips that learned more than they taught. Pulpits swapped; choirs blended; visas were fought for with lawyers on retainer. The Black church became more visibly global, even when its address stayed local.

Environmental justice and the parish ecology

Congregations mapped air quality, truck routes, heat islands, and flood plains over their parish maps. Sermons on stewardship gained teeth: trees planted, cooling centers opened, solar arrays installed on flat roofs, lead lines replaced, zoning meetings attended. Youth preached climate laments; elders told stories of creeks now culverted; planners in pews designed pocket parks. The sacrament of water—baptism—met the politics of water—bills, pipes, and trust. The theology was old: creation as gift; neighbor as charge.[87]

Theological education retooled

Seminaries pivoted to access and relevance: hybrid degrees, evening cohorts for working adults, contextual education rooted in justice practice, and certificates for lay leaders running ministries as complex as small agencies. Curricula braided Bible, counseling, organizational leadership, finance, media, and policy. Field ed sites included shelters, startups, schools, and city agencies. The aim was practical holiness: heads trained without losing hearts, hearts on fire without burning out.

Scandals, repentance, repair

Public failures—financial misconduct, abuse of power, sexual harm—cut trust quickly. Better churches practiced immediate truth-telling, survivor-first care, independent investigations, and consequences that matched harm. Where possible, they pursued repair: funds for victims, public confession, leadership changes, and structural fixes to prevent repetition. The test was whether a church loved its people more than its reputation. The risk was institutional death; the hope was institutional conversion.

Death, grief, and the great pause

Pandemics and mass grief taught improvisation: virtual funerals, drive-by repasts, outdoor vigils, meal trains for widowers learning kitchens, tablets held at bedside for last goodbyes. When doors reopened, liturgies held lament longer; memorial walls stayed up longer; counseling lines lengthened. The doctrine of the communion of saints felt nearer. The church remembered its first vocation: to bury the dead and teach the living to hope.

Young adults: belonging before believing

For many under 35, the sequence inverted: belonging before believing, practice before doctrine. Churches that flourished made room to serve before membership, to ask before assent, to try small groups before public declaration. Service projects, book clubs, arts nights, and justice campaigns functioned as catechesis by doing. Clarity came later, not by pressure but by companionship and witness shaped by integrity and usefulness.[88]

Small church, big faith

Amid scale and screens, small congregations remained the miracle: a hundred people who know each other's names; a pastor who visits; a choir that lifts a room on three parts; deacons who fix a porch; a building that opens for every civic need because it is the only room on the block with chairs enough. Their budgets stretch; their calendars tire; their work is irreplaceable. When the grid goes down, they are the grid.

What endures

Across the era's arguments and accelerations, certain things endure. The word preached with care. The table set with reverence. The water poured with names. The song that holds the room. The hand on a shoulder in the hallway after hard news. The ledger kept honestly. The meeting that starts and ends when promised. The committee that remembers the least-loved and the most-forgotten. The prayer that says thank you for breath, for patience, for the chance to try again next week.

Looking forward

The next decades will keep testing resilience: artificial intelligence reshaping work; climate stress moving families; politics fraying local trust; new diasporas changing language and habit; and the constant risk of cynicism smothering care. The path forward will likely look like the best of the past, adapted: parish attention with global imagination; sacrament with strategy; confession with repair; art with argument; and the steady insistence that faith is not a private temperature but a public way of life—with addresses, budgets, names, and a song strong enough to teach courage to children not yet born.

From that truth—the conviction that faith is not a private temperature but a public way of life—with addresses, budgets, names, and a song strong enough to teach courage to children not yet born—flows the long story we have traced in this book. The arc is neither accidental nor finished. It begins, as Chapter 1 reminded us, on a desert road where an Ethiopian treasurer, a reader of scripture and a traveler between worlds, paused long enough to meet the gospel and carry it back into the life of his people. His was a small, decisive crossing of borders: a moment when faith became a thread binding distant places into a common story.

That same braided thread runs through slave cabins and sanctified halls, through Freedom Rides and sit-ins, through revival tents and voting booths. Today it lengthens again, not by camel or schooner but by fiber-optic cables and satellite dishes—digital churches broadcasting sermons into kitchens and dorm rooms, podcasts translating spiritual counsel into earbuds, global networks convening worshipers in Lagos, London, and Louisville at once. The Ethiopian treasurer's journey is mirrored in these migrations of song and scripture: translation, reception, and the making of a holy commons that refuses to be contained.

Black churches remain a source of sanctuary and strategy, grief and rejoicing, relief and renaissance. They shoulder material needs—food pantries, after-school programs, housing initiatives—while shaping moral imagination in the public square. Their prophets continue to call out injustice, their teachers forge leaders, and their artists make beauty that interrupts despair. The challenges are real—economic strain, congregational aging, political polarization, and the seductions and inequalities of new technology—but so are the opportunities: innovation in ministry, global solidarity, intergenerational renewal, and creative partnerships across faiths and movements.

If history has taught us anything, it is that endurance is not passive. It is practiced in hymnbooks and ledgers, in bold sermons and tender pastoral visits, in litigation and in bedside prayers. The story of Christian Black America is not merely a chronicle of suffering and triumph; it is a covenant of work and witness. May the churches we have honored here continue to steward their addresses and budgets, to remember every name, and to sing a song that will teach courage to those not yet born—carrying forward an ancient light into an uncertain but hopeful tomorrow.

Endnotes

1. Biblical quotations and patristic references use standard English translations (NRSV/ESV for Scripture; NPNF series for early church writers unless otherwise noted).

2.

3. "Candace" as a royal title (Kandake): Strabo, Geography 17.1.54; Pliny the Elder, Natural History 6.186. For the title and queenship, see László Török, The Kingdom of Kush: Handbook of the Napatan-Meroitic Civilization (1997), and Derek A. Welsby, The Kingdom of Kush (1996).

4. Identification of the Kandake in Acts with Amanitore (variant spellings Amanitere/Amanitore), a reigning queen of Meroë in the 1st c. CE: Török (1997), 495–505; Welsby (1996), 195–207.

5. Meroitic trade, administration, and literacy: Bruce Trigger et al., Ancient Egypt: A Social History (1983), 307–12; Ranel R. MacIver & C. Leonard Woolley, The City of Meroe (1911); M. Shinnie, Ancient Nubia (1954).

6. Amanirenas' war with Rome; sources and archaeology: Strabo, Geography 17.1.54; Pliny, NH 6.186; S. Quirke & J. Spencer (eds.), The British Museum Book of Ancient Egypt (1992), re: bronze head of Augustus from Meroë (BM 1911,0901.1).

7. Simon of Cyrene (Mark 15:21; Matt 27:32; Luke 23:26); Lucius of Cyrene (Acts 13:1); Rufus (Rom 16:13). On diaspora Cyrene and early Christian networks, see Shaye J. D. Cohen, From the Maccabees to the Mishnah (1987).

8. Patristic treatments of the Ethiopian: John Chrysostom, Homilies on the Acts of the Apostles (esp. Hom. XIX on Acts 8); Augustine, Sermon 134; Origen, Homilies on Luke and Acts fragments (for method).

9. Septuagint origins: Letter of Aristeas (tradition) with critical framing in Timothy Michael Law, When God Spoke Greek (2013).

10. Eusebius on Mark and Anianus in Alexandria: Ecclesiastical History 2.16.

11. Foundational setting: Philo of Alexandria, e.g., On the Creation; On the Migration of Abraham (allegory and diaspora Judaism).

12. *(Kom el-Dikka sector, Polish Centre of Mediterranean Archaeology, seasons 1960s–1990s; preliminary notices 1969–1974)*

13. Eusebius, Hist. Eccl. 5.10–11

14. Catechetical school figures: Pantaenus (Eusebius, HE 5.10–11) ; Clement of Alexandria, Stromata 1.5; 6.8; Origen, On First Principles (De Principiis) 1.1.6; 4.2.2–4; selections in Rowan Greer (t rans.), Origen: An Exhortation to Martyrdom, Prayer, and Selected Works (1979).

15. **Origen, On First Principles (De Principiis) 1.1.6; 4.2.2–4**: Origen's influential method of interpretation is described: "The divine Scriptures have a body, a soul, and a spirit."

16. (Pre-Nicene Alexandrian trajectory; see Athanasius, De Decretis; Orations against the Arians)

17. Alexandrian Christology and later Nicene language: Athanasius, De Decretis; Orations Against the Arians; Khaled Anatolios, Retrieving Nicaea (2011).

18. Early Christian domestic spaces in Alexandria: PCMA field reports; Iwona Zych (ed.), Alexandria: The Auditoria on Kom el-Dikka (various seasons.

19. Tertullian: Apologeticus (esp. ch. 50 for the oft-paraphrased "the blood of the martyrs is seed"); Adversus Praxean (Trinity, substantia/persona). See Geoffrey D. Dunn (ed.), Tertullian (Routledge, 2004); Eric Osborn, Tertullian, First Theologian of the West (1997).

20. Origen: Eusebius, HE 6; On First Principles; Hexapla (fragments). Ronald E. Heine (trans.), Origen: Homilies on Genesis and Exodus; Henri Crouzel, Origen (1989).

21. Athanasius: De Incarnatione 54.3 ("He became man that we might become god"); Council of Nicaea (325) and homoousios; Khaled Anatolios, Athanasius (2004); Timothy D. Barnes, Athanasius and Constantius (1993).

22. Carthage and Latin Christianity: J. H. S. Burleigh, Church History of North Africa (1953); David Wilhite, Tertullian the African (2011).

23. Frumentius and Aedesius: Rufinus, Ecclesiastical History 1.9–10 (trans. P. L. Schaff, NPNF series).

24. Athanasius' role in consecrating Frumentius: Athanasius, Apologia ad Constantium; Letters; W. C. Bond, The Early Ethiopian Church (1964).

25. Ezana's conversion; inscriptions and coinage: Stuart Munro-Hay, Aksum: An African Civilization of Late Antiquity (1991); Wolfgang Hahn & Vincent West, Sylloge of Aksumite Coins (2010); RIE (Recueil des inscriptions de l'Éthiopie ancienne), vols. 1–2.

26. "Lord of Heaven" phrasing and Christian titulature in Ezana's inscriptions: RIE 189–190; J. Drewes in RIE.

27. Ge'ez Bible and liturgy; Nine Saints tradition: Sergew Hable-Selassie, Ancient and Medieval Ethiopian History (1972); Taddesse Tamrat, Church and State in Ethiopia (1972).

28. Kebra Nagast (The Glory of Kings): E. A. Wallis Budge (trans., 1922) with critical reassessments in Edward Ullendorff, Ethiopia and the Bible (1968).

29. Miaphysite alignment and Alexandrian ties: Aziz S. Atiya, A History of Eastern Christianity (1968).

30. "Pupil-smiters" (rumāt al-ḥadaq) description of Nubian archers: Arabic chronicles summarized in Welsby (2002), 20–29.

31. Arab-Nubian conflicts and the Baqt treaty (652): al-Balādhurī, Futūḥ al-Buldān; Ibn 'Abd al-Hakam, Futūḥ Miṣr; Ibn Salīm al-Aswānī (as preserved in al-Maqrīzī), with analysis in Derek A. Welsby, The Medieval Kingdoms of Nubia (2002), and William Y. Adams, Nubia: Corridor to Africa (1977).

32. Faras (Pakhoras) Cathedral frescoes; UNESCO salvage: Kazimierz Michałowski, Faras: The Wall Paintings (1974); Stefan Jakobielski, Christian Nubia at the Height of Its Civilization (2001); National Museum in Warsaw and Sudan National Museum catalogs.

33. Dongola and Qasr Ibrim archaeology: W. Y. Adams, Qasr Ibrim: The Ballaña Phase (1996); Polish Centre of Mediterranean Archaeology reports on Dongola (Włodzimierz Godlewski).

34. Old Nubian language and manuscripts: Gerald M. Browne, Old Nubian Grammar (1989); Vincent W. J. van Gerven Oei, A Reference Grammar of Old Nubian (2021).

35. Royal titulature (Merkurios, Georgios) and ecclesiastical art: Welsby (2002), 80–141; Jakobielski (2001).

36. "Invisible institution," ring shout, and hush harbors: Albert J. Raboteau, Slave Religion (1978); Sterling Stuckey, Slave Culture (1987); Katrina Dyonne Thompson, Ring Shout, Wheel About (2014).

37. Atlantic catechesis and baptisms near forts; Kongo Christianity: John K. Thornton, The Kongolese Saint Anthony (1998); Linda M. Heywood & John K. Thornton, Central Africans, Atlantic Creoles, and the Foundation of the Americas, 1585–1660 (2007).

38. Shipboard and plantation religion testimonies: Olaudah Equiano, Interesting Narrative (1789); WPA Slave Narratives; Raboteau (1978).

39. Spirituals as biblical exegesis in song: Eileen Southern, The Music of Black Americans (1971); James H. Cone, The Spirituals and the Blues (1972).

40. "Slave Bible" (Parts of the Holy Bible, Selected for the Use of the Negro Slaves in the British West-India Islands, c. 1807/1808): see Museum of the Bible/Fisk University exhibit materials; Vincent Wimbush (ed.), African Americans and the Bible (2000).

41. Praise houses and hush arbors in the Lowcountry: Margaret Washington Creel, "A Peculiar People" (1988); Charles Joyner, Down by the Riverside (1984)

42. Call-and-response/"people's commentary": Raboteau (1978); James Abbington (ed.), Readings in African American Church Music (2001).

43. Watch Night (Moravian/Methodist origins; 1862 Emancipation vigils): Sylvester A. Johnson, African American Religions, 1500–2000 (2015), 147–49; Lean'tin Bracks & Jessie Carney Smith, Black Women and the Mission of Watch Night (overview).

44. Revival religion and enslaved conversions: Sylvia R. Frey & Betty Wood, Come Shouting to Zion (1998).

45. Early Black exhorters and class meetings: Milton C. Sernett, Black Religion and American Evangelicalism (1975); W. E. B. Du Bois, The Souls of Black Folk (1903), "Of the Faith of the Fathers."

46. "Two pulpits in one room" (segregated seating): Albert J. Raboteau, A Fire in the Bones (1995), ch. 2.

47. Denmark Vesey: Douglas R. Egerton, He Shall Go Out Free (1999).

48. Nat Turner: Patrick H. Breen, The Land Shall Be Deluged in Blood (2015); Thomas R. Gray, The Confessions of Nat Turner (1831).

49. St. George's (Philadelphia) incident; Free African Society: Richard Allen, The Life, Experience, and Gospel Labours (1833); Minutes of the Free African Society (1787–1792).

50. Absalom Jones and St. Thomas African Episcopal Church: "A Narrative of the Proceedings of the Black People During the Late Awful Calamity..." (Allen & Jones, 1794); Gary B. Nash, Forging Freedom (1988).

51. Bethel AME property struggle; 1816 AME organization: Richard S. Newman, Freedom's Prophet: Bishop Richard Allen (2008); Dennis C. Dickerson, A History of the AME Church (2020).

52. Early Black Baptists (Petersburg First Baptist; Gillfield): Albert J. Raboteau (1995), 78–92; Benjamin E. Mays & Joseph W. Nicholson, The Negro's Church (1933).

53. Vigilance committees/Underground Railroad networks: Eric Foner, Gateway to Freedom (2015); Cheryl Janifer LaRoche, Free Black Communities and the Underground Railroad (2014).

54. Biblical arguments vs. "curse of Ham": David M. Goldenberg, The Curse of Ham (2003).

55. Press and petitioning: The Christian Recorder (AME), The Colored American, Frederick Douglass' Paper; see John W. Blassingame (ed.), Slave Testimony (1977).

56. Women's aid and church-based logistics: Julie Roy Jeffrey, The Great Silent Army of Abolitionism (1998).

57. Church building and expansion; denominational growth: Dennis C. Dickerson (2020); Sandy Dwayne Martin, Black Baptists and African Missions (1989).

58. Women's boards and benevolence: Evelyn Brooks Higginbotham, Righteous Discontent (1993).

59. Freedmen's Bureau partnerships; education: Eric Foner, Reconstruction (1988); James D. Anderson, The Education of Blacks in the South, 1860–1935 (1988); Heather Andrea Williams, Self-Taught (2005).

60. Union Leagues and political education: Michael W. Fitzgerald, Splendid Failure (2007); Steven Hahn, A Nation Under Our Feet (2003).

61. Church press and minutes: The Christian Recorder; Star of Zion; National Baptist Convention minutes (various).

62. Great Migration scale: Isabel Wilkerson, The Warmth of Other Suns (2010); James R. Grossman, Land of Hope (1989).

63. Olivet Baptist (Chicago) and Black metropolis: St. Clair Drake & Horace Cayton, Black Metropolis (1945); Allan H. Spear, Black Chicago (1967).

64. Urban congregational hubs: Wallace D. Best, Passionately Human, No Less Divine (2005); Shane White & Graham White, Harlem's Pastor: The Life of Adam Clayton Powell, Sr. (2014).

65. Temperance, public health, and church clinics: Evelyn Brooks Higginbotham (1993), ch. 4–6; W. E. B. Du Bois, The Philadelphia Negro (1899); Vanessa Northington Gamble, Making a Place for Ourselves (1995).

66. Women's leadership: Nannie Helen Burroughs, speeches/writings; Anthea Butler, Women in the Church of God in Christ (2007); Bettye Collier-Thomas, Jesus, Jobs, and Justice (2010); Sarah Mapps Douglass: Margaret Hope Bacon, But One Race (2002).

67. NACW and settlement work: Anne Firor Scott, Natural Allies (1991).

68. Mortality and WCTU membership context: city health reports (1890s); WCTU Annual Reports (late 19th c.).

69. Church infrastructure in the civil-rights movement: Aldon D. Morris, The Origins of the Civil Rights Movement (1984); Charles Marsh, God's Long Summer (1997).

70. Nonviolence training (James Lawson; SNCC/SCLC): David Halberstam, The Children (1998); Taylor Branch, Parting the Waters (1988).

71. Music of the movement: Bernice Johnson Reagon, If You Don't Go, Don't Hinder Me (2007); Freedom Song collections.

72. Legal logistics and bail funds: Branch (1988–2006 trilogy); Clayborne Carson (ed.), The Papers of Martin Luther King, Jr.

73. Bombings, funerals, and sacred protest: Diane McWhorter, Carry Me Home (2001); Glenn T. Eskew, But for Birmingham (1997).

74. Black theology: James H. Cone, Black Theology and Black Power (1969); A Black Theology of Liberation (1970); Gayraud Wilmore, Black Religion and Black Radicalism (1972; rev. eds.).

75. Ethics from intent to impact; public theology: Luke Bretherton, Christianity and Contemporary Politics (2010) for method.

76. African contextual theologies: Allan Boesak, Black and Reformed (1984); Itumeleng Mosala, Biblical Hermeneutics and Black Theology (1989); Mercy Amba Oduyoye, Daughters of Anowa (1995).

77. Megachurch trends: Scott Thumma & Dave Travis, Beyond Megachurch Myths (2007); Hartford Institute for Religion Research, "Megachurches Today" surveys (2000s–2020s).

78. Disaffiliation and young adults: Pew Research Center, Religious Landscape Studies (2014, 2019); PRRI, American Values Atlas (various); Robert D. Putnam & David E. Campbell, American Grace (2010).

79. AI, tech ethics, and ministry: Shannon Vallor, Technology and the Virtues (2016); church tech/ethics primers (Ecclesial/denominational white papers); ACM Code of Ethics (context for data/AI).

80. Digital worship/COVID-19 pivot: Pew Research Center, "How the Coronavirus Has — and Hasn't — Changed the Way Americans Worship" (2020–2021); Barna Group, State of the Church (2020).

81. Case leaders: T. D. Jakes (The Potter's House); Creflo Dollar (World Changers); Eddie L. Long (New Birth). For prosperity currents: Kate Bowler, Blessed: A History of the American Prosperity Gospel (2013).

82. Accountability/governance in large churches: Warren Bird & Scott Thumma, The Other 80 Percent (2011); public reporting on scandals as cautionary case material (news archives).

83. Digital worship/COVID-19 pivot: Pew Research Center, "How the Coronavirus Has — and Hasn't — Changed the Way Americans Worship" (2020–2021); Barna Group, State of the Church (2020).

84. Global Black Christianity and diaspora churches (RCCG, etc.) : Asonzeh Ukah, A New Paradigm of Pentecostal Power (2008); Ruth Marshall, Political Spiritualities (2009); Adeshina Afolayan & Toyin Falola (eds.), Pentecostalism in Africa (2018).

85. Mental health and Black churches: Harold G. Koenig, Handbook of Religion and Health (2nd ed., 2012); Thema Bryant-Davis (clinical-pastoral resources); NAMI FaithNet materials.

86. LGBTQ+ debates in Black churches: The Fellowship of Affirming Ministries (organizational materials); COGIC and AME statements (discipline/Doctrines & Discipline); Yvette A. Flunder, Where the Edge Gathers (2005); J. Kameron Carter & Anthony B. Pinn (eds.), The Oxford Handbook of African American Theology (2014) for survey.

87. Environmental justice and parish ecology: Robert D. Bullard, Dumping in Dixie (1990); Hilda Kurtz et al., Black Churches and Environmental Justice (case studies).

88. "Belonging before believing" and missional praxis: Michael Frost & Alan Hirsch, The Shaping of Things to Come (2003) — for the concept's contemporary framing.

About the author

Rene' Stanley

I've spent over four decades watching and participating in the digital revolution. From my first encounters with computer programming in high school during the late 1970s to navigating today's complex cyber landscape, technology has been a constant companion in my journey. While serving in the U.S. Army during Desert Storm, I witnessed firsthand how rapidly technology could evolve and transform our capabilities.

Now, as I navigate my senior years, I find myself in a unique position – someone who understands both the tremendous potential and the growing challenges of our digital age. This book represents not just my knowledge, but our shared experience as we continue to adapt and learn in this ever-changing digital world.

Through her writing, Rene' aims to illuminate the positive aspects of life's journey, drawing from her varied experiences to create stories that resonate with readers of all backgrounds.

Readers can discover more about Rene's work at www.books-by-rene.store

www.ingramcontent.com/pod-product-compliance
Lightning Source LLC
Chambersburg PA
CBHW060417130626
46555CB00005B/2096